# Sass n' SOUL

## LIVE AS THOUGH YOU ARE LEGEND

Not someday — right now, in the small,
soulful choices that shape your legacy.

**CONTACT US**
925-995-1120
Connect@CyndeePaulsonHeer.com
Editorial@SassNSoul.com
CyndeePaulsonHeer.com
www.thesassnsoullife.com

■ **SASS N' SOUL MAGAZINE** *DECEMBER 2025*

# TABLE *Of* CONTENTS

# I Just Was!

Standing there, hip out, hand on hip, I wasn't cocky; I was confident. I sought neither permission nor forgiveness for who I was or the passions that fueled me . . . It just was! . . . I just was!

I had yet to fall prey to the demands and rules of life. I only knew that whatever "it" was, I could do it. I had not yet learned to doubt myself. Surrounded by 4 brothers and their friends, I found my moxie. Unknowingly, in all my authenticity, I was shaping my own character with vision and volition.

## Such is the unencumbered freedom of a 5-year-old.

Welcome to Sass n' Soul, where your journey of authenticity, self-actualization, and success either begins or continues.

We're not just a magazine — we're a movement. Sass n' Soul is where wisdom meets wit, purpose meets passion, and women (and a few good men) come together to live and lead with intention.

Here, your story matters. Your voice is valued. Your growth — both personal and professional — is celebrated.

Within these pages, we share insights, inspiration, and real-life experiences to help you grow into the next authentic, unapologetic version of yourself.

Join the Sass n' Soul community and discover the transformative power of authenticity, collaboration, and conscious living. Because success isn't just about what you achieve — it's about who you become along the way.

## Write your story and Live Your Legend!

# TABLE *Of* CONTENTS

# BRAND PROMISE

To inspire. To empower.
To celebrate.

Every page, every story,
every voice reminds you
that you are both the
author and the legend of
your own becoming.

# TABLE *Of* CONTENTS

# WHAT WE STAND FOR

- Growth is a lifelong journey
- Evolution is your power.
- Authentic leadership elevates the collective.
- Purpose is lived through contribution.
- Connection fuels possibility.

# TABLE *Of* CONTENTS

# SASS N' SOUL MISSION

Sass n' Soul Magazine exists to help women — and a few good men — grow again and again into the next best version of themselves.

We champion authenticity, self-actualization, and purpose-driven living. Because legacy isn't just what you leave behind . . . someday — it's what you're creating right now with every action you take.

# TABLE *Of* CONTENTS

# You're Just Getting Started

**For Purpose-Driven Entrepreneurs with a Message**

You have expertise, experience, and wisdom that could genuinely help people.

Now you're ready to share it with the world, but something keeps stopping you.

## Join The Impact Messaging Lab

**FREE TRIAL**

- Monthly challenges that turn your lived experience into magnetic messaging
- Get practical support, not just theory about "finding your voice"
- Get accountabiity and support with virtual co-working and office hours

Monthly membership. Cancel anytime

**For More Information**
https://impactmessaginglab.substack.com/sassnsoul

# TABLE *Of* CONTENTS

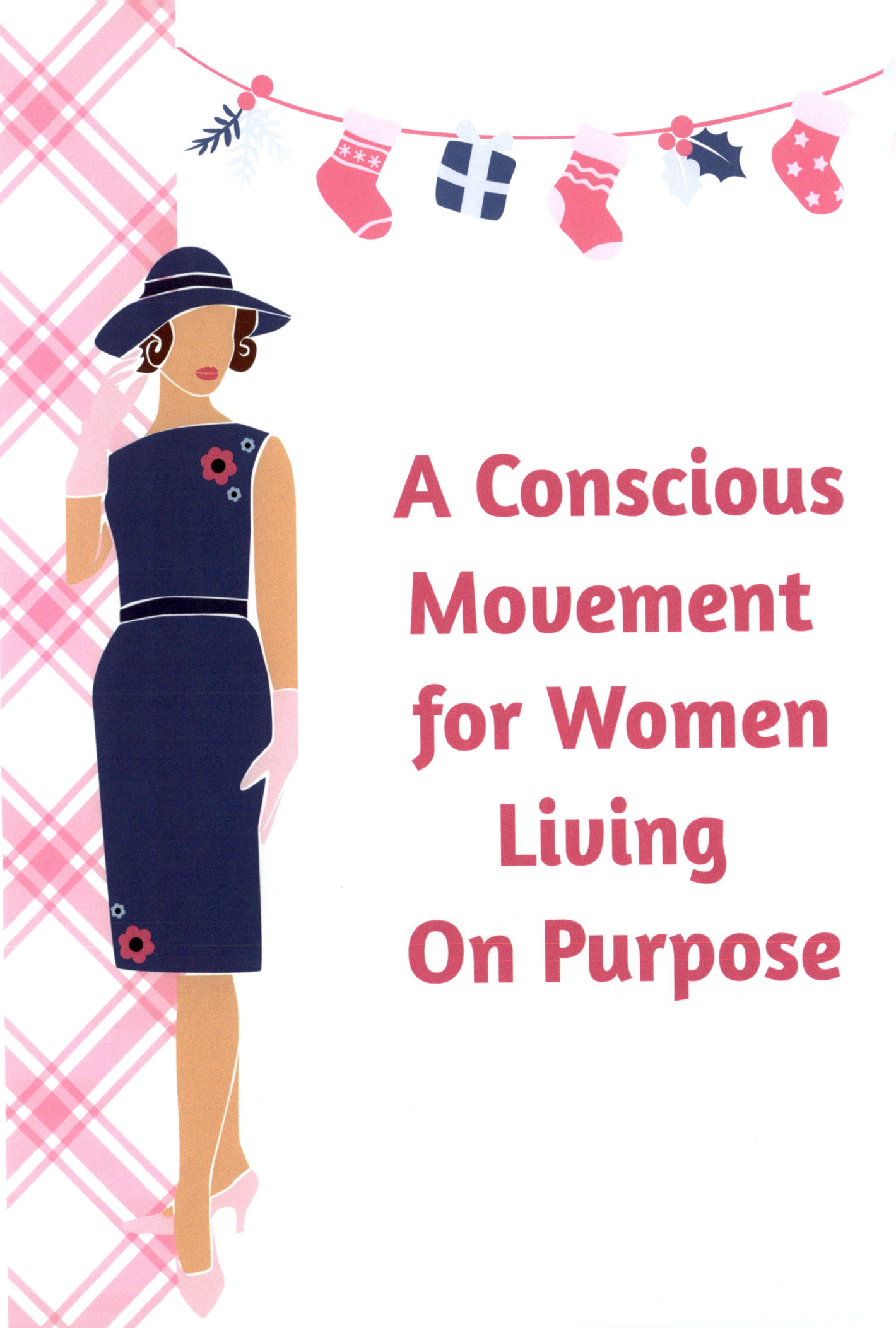

# A Conscious Movement for Women Living On Purpose

**Cyndee Paulson-Heer**
Founder at Sass n' Soul
TheSassNSoulLife.com

# AUTHENTIC LEADERSHIP: LEADING FROM THE HEART

By Cyndee Paulson-Heer

While the concept of Authentic Leadership is still toddling about it is growing in popularity. Once, a widely misinterpreted and often mocked concept, many people, young and old, have come to respect the Authentic Leadership style. At Sass n' Soul, we believe that authenticity is the key to creating a thriving and meaningful life, personally and professionally.

Authentic Leadership is about leading with heart and purpose. Rather than chasing superficial wins, it emphasizes integrity, responsibility, and a steadfast commitment to morality and principles. Authentic leaders are introspective, continuously taking stock of themselves and striving for personal growth. Leaders focus on becoming the person they ask their team or family to emulate.

True authentic leaders align their actions with their core values and mission, fostering trust within their circle of influence. They are approachable, inspiring, and motivational, creating an environment that encourages growth and bold risk-taking—key ingredients for unlocking brilliance and innovation.

What truly sets Authentic Leadership apart is the intention driving their actions. Authentic leaders consistently seek the highest and best outcomes for everyone involved—not just for themselves or their teams, but for the collective good. Their leadership is a journey of connection, purpose, and positive impact.

**Core Traits of an Authentic Leader**
Authentic Leadership isn't just about leading others—it's about leading yourself first. Here are some key traits that set authentic leaders apart:

**1. Commitment to Self-Improvement**
Authentic leaders are life-long learners. They prioritize continuous self-evolution, recognizing that personal development is a lifelong journey. By investing in personal development, they build confidence, enhance their skills, and strengthen their leadership abilities.

**2. Cultivate Self-Awareness**
Self-awareness is at the heart of Authentic Leadership.

By reflecting on one's strengths, values, and experiences, authentic leaders cultivate emotional intelligence, enabling them to connect meaningfully with others and lead effectively.

### 3. Discipline in Action
Self-aware leaders translate their knowledge into action. They ensure their decisions and behaviors align with their values, reinforcing trust and credibility in their leadership.

### 4. Mission-Driven Leadership
Authentic leaders are guided by a sense of purpose rooted in their values. This mission not only fuels their own drive but also inspires those they lead to find fulfillment and success in their goals and lives.

### 5. Inspiring Trust
Trust is a core element of Authentic Leadership. It is essential in building meaningful relationships. It creates a foundation of safety and openness, enabling individuals to collaborate, innovate, and contribute. Without trust, communication breaks down, engagement falters, and progress stalls, making it an essential element for a "thrive environment."

### The Benefits of Authentic Leadership
Authentic Leadership is as relevant for the CEO of a thriving business as it is for the founder shaping a vision or the leader of a family. Its principles create transformative, universally applicable outcomes by fostering trust, connection, and purpose in every facet of life.

### 1. Increased Trust and Loyalty
Authentic leaders build trust through transparency and consistent actions that align with their values. Their integrity cultivates loyalty, strengthening relationships and creating collaborative environments where people feel secure and valued.

### 2. Improved Communication
By fostering openness and clarity in their goals and values, authentic leaders create spaces where family and team members feel encouraged to share ideas, voice concerns, and collaborate effectively. This reduces misunderstandings,

*"Lead with integrity, act with purpose, and you don't just change outcomes—you change people."*

builds alignment toward shared objectives, and improves communication.

### 3. Higher Engagement and Empowerment
By caring about individuals and fostering personal growth, authentic leaders inspire deeper connections. By empowering individuals to take ownership of their roles and contribute their unique skills, authentic leaders encourage their families and teams to engage and make impactful, meaningful contributions.

### 4. Stronger Culture
Authentic leaders model the values they wish to see, fostering an environment of trust, respect, and alignment. This culture encourages collaboration, reduces conflict, and creates a shared sense of purpose within the team or family.

### 5. Better Decision-Making
Self-awareness and a commitment to ethical standards enable authentic leaders to make thoughtful decisions that align with both short-term goals and long-term values. These decisions build credibility and strengthen trust in their leadership.

### 6. Greater Innovation and Creativity
By fostering diverse perspectives and safe spaces for new ideas, authentic leaders encourage creativity and risk-taking, driving innovation and team growth. Families and teams feel empowered to share new ideas in a safe environment, driving progress and growth.

### 7. Stronger Relationships and Team Dynamics
Empathy and vulnerability help leaders build trust and create bonds within families and teams, encouraging collaboration and inclusiveness for stronger outcomes.

### 8. Resilience and Adaptability

Grounded in their core values, authentic leaders navigate challenges with integrity, modeling resilience and adaptability. Their ability to adapt to change without compromising their vision inspires confidence and stability.

### 9. Higher Well-Being

Authentic leaders prioritize the well-being of those they lead, encouraging balance and healthier environments. By supporting work-life harmony, they foster a culture that promotes both personal and professional fulfillment.

### 10. Better Talent Retention

When people feel valued, supported, and encouraged to grow, they are more likely to remain loyal. In the workplace, authentic leadership reduces turnover by cultivating a sense of belonging and providing opportunities for personal and professional development.

### 11. Sustained Impact

Authentic Leadership creates a legacy of positive change. By inspiring others to embrace authenticity, these leaders drive meaningful, lasting results that extend beyond their immediate influence.

### The Transformative Power of Authentic Leadership

Authentic Leadership is more than a leadership style—it's a way of being that has the power to transform individuals, teams, families, and organizations. By leading with integrity, empathy, and purpose, authentic leaders create environments where people feel valued, connected, and inspired. They cultivate trust, drive innovation, and build cultures rooted in mutual respect and shared values.

In a world often driven by short-term gains and surface-level wins, authentic leadership stands out as a beacon of hope and possibility. It reminds us that true success isn't measured solely by achievements or titles but by the impact we make and the legacy we weave and leave. Authentic leaders don't just lead—they uplift, empower, and inspire others to embrace their own authenticity and potential.

At Sass n' Soul, we believe the world is craving authenticity and connection and we are deeply in need of more leaders who are willing to lead with their hearts, align their actions

with their values, and create meaningful change. And dare I repeat: Whether you're the CEO of a global company, a founder shaping your vision, or the leader of your family, the principles of Authentic Leadership are universally relevant and profoundly transformative.

By embracing Authentic Leadership, you're not just shaping outcomes—you're shaping lives. You're creating a future built on trust, meaningful connections, and shared values. In doing so, you're leaving a legacy that extends into the future, and inspires others to their higher purpose. Authentic leadership isn't just important—it's essential for building a more empowered, resilient, and compassionate world.

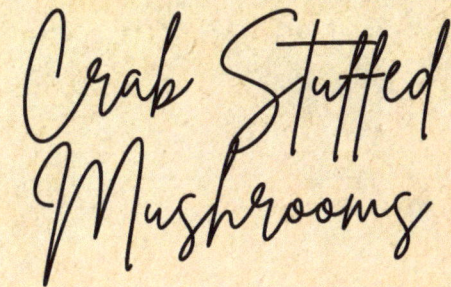

# Crab Stuffed Mushrooms

**From the Kitchen of:**
*Sally Jean Longwell-vonHofen-Thomas*
*Compliments of Sally and Chuck vonHofen*

## Ingredients:

- 12 large or 24 medium mushrooms (white mushrooms or baby bella's, your preference).
- 2 tablespoons minced green onions
- 5 tablespoons butter
- 1 teaspoon lemon juice
- 1 cup (about 8 ounces) flaked, cooked crab meat (diced shrimp also works)
- ½ cup soft bread crumbs (about 1 slice of white or sourdough bread, whirled in a blender).
- 1 egg, slightly beaten
- ½ teaspoon dill weed
- ¾ cup shredded Montery Jack cheese (pepper jack is a great alternative).
- ¼ cup dry white wine
- Lemon wedges

## Directions:

- Remove stems from whole, cleaned mushrooms. Chop stems and saute them with the onions in 2 tablespoons of the butter. When onions are limp, add the lemon juice, crab or shrimp, bread crumbs, egg, dill weed, and ¼ cup of the cheese.
- Melt the remaining 3 tablespoons butter in a 9x13 pan. Turn the mushroom caps in this butter to coat them. Spoon 2 tablespoons of the filling into each mushroom cap. Place the filled mushrooms in the buttered pan. Sprinkle with remaining cheese. Pour the white wine into the bottom of the pan.
- Bake in a 400 degree oven for 15 to 20 minutes. Serve hot with lemon wedges. Makes about 6 servings. (Makes an excellent dinner with spinach salad and a sourdough baguette).

**Diana Concoff-Morgan**
Founder of Whole Heart Marketing™

# AUTHENTICITY IS THE NEW ALGORITHM: TAKE BACK YOUR ONLINE PRESENCE FROM AI

By Diana Concoff Morgan

In a world suddenly flooded with AI-generated everything, the real luxury online is *being real*. Authenticity — your true voice, your lived experience, your unique energy — has never been more valuable. Yet, for many women entrepreneurs, the digital noise has made it harder than ever to be heard.

We've entered an era where content can be created in seconds, but connection still takes time and heart.

### The Rise of the Generic Brand

Let's be honest: it's easy to let AI take over. It promises speed, polish, and *"perfectly optimized"* posts. But what's happening quietly beneath that convenience is a slow dilution of originality. When we let algorithms dictate our words, our online presence starts to sound like everyone else's. The rhythm flattens. The spark dims. The subtle, soulful touch that only *you* can bring begins to disappear.

AI learns from what already exists. That means the more it creates, the more it repeats — until authenticity becomes the rarest voice in the feed. And for heart-centered entrepreneurs, that sameness can feel like betrayal.

We didn't start our businesses to sound like a bot. We started them to make a difference, to inspire, to connect.

### Authenticity Is the New Currency

Your audience isn't looking for perfection — they're looking for presence.

They want to know there's a real woman behind the brand — one who feels, reflects, stumbles, learns, and keeps showing up anyway.

Authenticity online isn't about oversharing or showing every flaw. It's about alignment — when what you believe, what you say, and how you show up all match. That's when people trust you.

Ask yourself:

- Does my voice sound like me when I'm at my best — grounded, wise, and human?
- Does my audience feel my passion, not just my professionalism?
- Am I engaging to connect, or just to keep up?

Your brand's energy can't be faked. It's what makes your presence magnetic — and it's the one thing AI will never be able to imitate.

### The Feminine Edge: Connection Over Automation

There's a reason women are leading the movement back toward authentic marketing. The feminine way of creating – relational, intuitive, empathic – is the antidote to the AI takeover.

- Where automation relies on data, intuition relies on wisdom.
- Where algorithms chase attention, women build trust.
- Where bots speak to everyone, we speak to *someone*.

That's the edge.

The energy of your words matters as much as the words themselves. When your intention is to uplift, connect, or contribute, people *feel* that. It's subtle, but it's real – and it's what turns followers into friends, and clients into community.

### The Soul of Your Brand

Here's the secret: your brand isn't just your logo, your colors, or your tagline. It's how people feel when they encounter you – online or off. It's the moment someone reads your post and thinks, "She gets me." It's the quiet recognition that you're not just selling something – you're *sharing* something.

In a world obsessed with faster, your presence slows people down. In a world craving connection, your authenticity gives them hope.

AI can amplify your message, but only if the message comes from your heart first.

### Take Back the Mic

We are living in a moment where machines can mimic our words – but never our wisdom.

Your job isn't to compete with AI. It's to be so deeply human that no technology can keep up.

So, the next time you open your laptop, don't ask, "What should I post today?"

Ask instead: "Who needs to hear what I have to say?" Because your brand is authenticity.

Your presence is your power. And that is something no algorithm can replicate.

*"Your job isn't to compete with AI. It's to be so deeply human that no technology can keep up."*

**Diana Concoff Morgan** *is a Conscious Digital Impact Strategist, author, and international speaker, who empowers entrepreneurs to grow their reach through authentic connection. Founder of Whole Heart Marketing™, she teaches strategies that turn relationships and referrals into clients—helping purpose-driven professionals use digital platforms consciously to expand their impact and influence.*

### Connect With Diana

www.facebook.com/WholeHeartMarketing
www.facebook.com/groups/wholeheartmarketing
withdianaconcoffmorgan
www.instagram.com/dianaconcoffmorgan
www.linkedin.com/in/dianaconcoffmorgan
www.twitter.com/dianarcmorgan
www.pinterest.com/dianacmorgan
www.youtube.com/dianaconcoffmorgan

**Ria**

# THE BASICS OF TAROT: A BEGINNER'S GUIDE

By Ria

Tarot has long carried an air of mystery. Some see it as a fortune-telling trick, others as a sacred spiritual practice, and many as something in between. But at its heart, Tarot is much simpler and more useful than myths make it out to be. The Major Arcana represent the universal archetypes and transformative themes of human existence, while the Minor Arcana depict the everyday experiences and practical circumstances that shape our lives—more below. They can reflect our thoughts, emotions, and choices back to us. Together, they mirror back our inner world—thoughts, emotions, and choices—illuminating what hides in the shadows and pointing us toward possibilities we may have overlooked.

Whether you're curious about diving in for the first time or just want to understand what all the fuss is about, here are some essentials that can help you better understand Tarot.

## A Brief History

Tarot didn't start as a mystical practice. In fact, the earliest Tarot decks appeared in 15th-century Europe as playing cards used for a game called *tarocchi*. It wasn't until the 18th and 19th centuries that people began using Tarot for divination and spiritual exploration.

Today, Tarot has grown into a versatile tool used by seekers, writers, coaches, and everyday people for self-reflection, guidance, and creative inspiration.

## What's in a Tarot Deck?

A standard Tarot deck has **78 cards**, divided into two main sections:

- **Major Arcana (22 cards):** These represent the big themes and life lessons—think archetypes like The Fool (new beginnings), The Lovers (relationships and choices), and Death (transformation, not literal death).
- **Minor Arcana (56 cards):** These cover day-to-day experiences. They're divided into four suits, much like a regular deck of cards:
  - **Wands** - action, creativity, passion
  - **Cups** - emotions, intuition, relationships
  - **Swords** - thoughts, clarity, challenges
  - **Pentacles** - work, finances, material world

Each suit has numbered cards (Ace through 10) and four court cards—Page, Knight, Queen, and King—which often represent personalities, roles, or aspects of ourselves.

## How Tarot Works

Here's the secret: Tarot doesn't *predict* your future. Instead, it works through **symbolism and intuition**. Each card is filled with imagery that taps into universal human experiences. When you draw cards for a question or situation, you interpret the images through your own lens, which often surfaces insights you already hold but hadn't quite put your finger on. The "magic" comes in believing you are pulling the right cards for your query, and in trusting your ability, or the reader's ability, to interpret the cards.

## The Basics of Reading Tarot

If you're just starting, you don't need to master all 78 cards at once. Start simple:

- **Set an intention.** Ask a clear question or focus on an area of your life. (Example: "What energy should I bring into my week?")
- **Shuffle, cut, and draw.** Trust yourself—there's no wrong way.
- **Read with openness.** Notice what stands out in the imagery, and what words come in for you as you unpack the imagery and read traditional interpretations. Compare the interpretation and don't ignore your gut response.

## Easy Spreads for Beginners

- **One-card pull:** Great for daily reflection.
- **Three-card spread:** Often used for past-present-future or situation-challenge-advice.
- **Celtic Cross:** A 10-card spread for deeper dives (more advanced, once you're comfortable).

Tip: Keep a Tarot journal. Write down your card pulls and how they connected to your day—you'll be surprised how quickly patterns emerge.

## Ethics & Best Practices

Tarot should empower, not frighten. Here are a few golden rules:

- Tarot offers guidance, not absolute answers.
- Avoid "yes/no" or fatalistic questions—focus instead on growth and perspective.
- Respect boundaries: don't read for others without their consent.
- Use Tarot as a tool for reflection, understanding and expansion, not as a crutch for every decision.

## Everyday Uses for Tarot

You don't need to be a mystic to make Tarot part of your life. People use the cards for:

- **Journaling prompts:** Pull a card and write about how its imagery or traditional interpretation relates to your current mood or goals. Beyond serving as a prompt, this practice will help you connect with the cards and deepen your understanding of them.
- **Creativity:** Writers and artists often use Tarot to spark ideas or overcome blocks.
- **Mindfulness:** Drawing a card in the morning can serve as a daily meditation or intention theme.
- **Personal growth:** Tarot can help identify patterns, highlight blind spots, and clarify choices.

## Getting Started

If you're ready to try Tarot, here are a few tips:

- **Choose a deck you connect with.** Many beginners start with the Rider-Waite-Smith deck, but I find it dated.
- **Use the guidebook—but don't cling to it.** Traditional meanings are helpful, but your intuition matters just as much, perhaps even more.
- **Practice regularly.** Like any skill, your understanding deepens and grows the more you work with it.
- **Stay curious.** Tarot is a lifelong journey, not a one-time trick.

## Final Thoughts

At its core, Tarot is about connection—connection to yourself, to your inner wisdom, and to the patterns of life that repeat in every human story. You don't need special powers to read the cards; you just need openness, curiosity, and a willingness to listen and learn.

So, the next time you shuffle a deck, remember: Tarot isn't telling you your fate. It's helping you see the road ahead a little more clearly—and reminding you that you hold the steering wheel.

**Fatina Bryan**

# DEBT-FREE DECEMBER: FIVE MOVES TO KEEP CREDIT CARDS FROM HIJACKING YOUR NEW YEAR

By Fatina Bryan

The holidays are magical—but they can also be expensive. Between travel, festive meals, and gifts that seem to multiply like elves, it's easy to wake up in January with a big-fat-gifting hangover and more credit card debt than sparkle. This can sure put a crimp in your New Year's cheer.

Here's the good news—staying out of debt doesn't mean cutting joy. It means being intentional. A few simple shifts can keep you financially free while still letting you celebrate big.

### 1. Set a Firm Holiday Budget Cap
Decide in advance what you're willing to spend—stick to it. Think of it as giving yourself the gift of peace. A budget is not a restriction—it's a protection.

### 2. Switch to Cash (or Debit) for Gifts
Research shows people spend less when they physically hand over cash instead of swiping a credit card. If you prefer plastic, use a debit card linked to a holiday account. If you don't already have one, you will promptly open this January. You won't overspend next year.

### 3. Give Experiences Instead of Expensive Things
Game nights, shared meals, or local adventures can cost less and mean more. Presence beats presents when it comes to making memories.

### 4. Prioritize Paying High-Interest Debt First
If you do put some holiday spending on credit, focus on paying off the highest-interest card as quickly as possible. With credit card interest rates gouging consumers the way they are, this one move alone can save buckets of money and quickly reduce stress.

### 5. Create a Holiday "Sinking Fund" for Next Year
Get ahead of "the holiday give." Create next year's Christmas budget now. Decide on a reasonable amount to allocate for holiday giving, divide the total by 12, and start saving in January. When December rolls around, viola, guilt-free gifting. Next year's holidays will already be funded, no stress required.

### A Mindset Reminder
Wealth isn't just about numbers in a bank account. It's also about feeling abundant.

Financial stress robs joy, and prolonged stress of any kind is bad for one's health. On the other hand, financial peace brings ease of mind and can promote joy in giving. This season, let your spending reflect your values and your income—not pressure, guilt, or comparison. Many individuals think that giving is love. I, absolutely LOVE giving. Staying within one's means is also love—it's self-love. So, as I taught my youngest son, some 25 years ago, when he wanted to spend his entire allowance on me for Mother's Day, "You allocate a smart percentage for gifting, stay within that budget, and everyone wins."

**Wrap-Up**
The holidays aren't meant to drain you; they're meant to delight you. With a few intentional choices and a bit of planning, you can protect your peace, safeguard your pocketbook, and step into the New Year debt-free.

Because the best holiday tradition is one you can afford to repeat.

# GIFTS WITH A RETURN

**Davie Singh**

By Davie Singh

The holidays bring out the best in us. We want to give generously, show love, and create lasting memories. But let's be honest—most of what gets wrapped in shiny paper ends up forgotten, broken, or donated somewhere down the road. What if this year you gave a gift that doesn't just sparkle for a season but grows in value for years to come?

That's the heart of wealth-building gifts. I wish someone had taught me this years ago: Wealth-building gifts are practical, purposeful, and deeply personal. When you choose to gift something that multiplies over time, you're giving more than money—you're passing on possibility and security.

### Why Wealth-Building Gifts Matter
Money itself is neutral. What we choose to do with it tells the story. For parents and grandparents, especially, financial gifts become a way to weave your values into the fabric of your family's future. Financial gifts say, *"I care about your tomorrow as much as your today."*

Think of it as *legacy in motion.* A $100 toy may bring joy for a month or even a year, but a $100 bond, stock, or savings contribution can add up over the years and open doors—five, ten, even twenty years down the road.

Those doors—education, opportunity, security—are far more meaningful than any toy tucked under a tree.

### Wealth-Building Gift Options
Here are a few ways to turn holiday generosity into lasting wealth:

### Savings Bonds & Treasuries
- The classic choice. They're safe, government-backed, and a good starter gift for children. Over time, they quietly grow, teaching patience and the power of compounding.

### Custodial Accounts (UGMA/UTMA)
- These accounts let you transfer stocks, bonds, or mutual funds to a minor. You control it until they're of age, benefiting from early exposure to investing.

### 529 College Savings Plans
- Education is one of the best investments. With tax-advantaged growth, your contribution today could one day pay for tuition, books, or even advanced training.

### Dividend-Paying Stocks or ETFs
- For teens and young adults, this can be exciting.

- Imagine gifting shares of a company they admire (like Disney or Apple). They not only watch their stock grow, but also earn dividends along the way.

## Life Insurance Policies
- It may not sound festive, but it's one of the most loving gifts you can give. It ensures protection for your family and builds a foundation of security.

## How to Make It Personal
The beauty of wealth-building gifts is that they're not just about numbers. Pair them with a story, a journal entry, or a handwritten note about *why* you chose this gift.

For example:
- "I bought you stock in Disney because I remember watching your eyes light up at your first Disneyland parade."
- "This savings bond is a seed. My wish is that you'll use this in the future to chase something bold or meaningful."

The financial piece grows with time—the sentiment lives on in memory.

## Teaching the Next Generation
Wealth-building gifts also offer teaching moments:
- Encourage kids to track the growth of their bond or stock
- Help teens set saving goals and celebrate milestones
- Use it as a conversation starter about values, choices, and long-term planning

You're not just giving money—you're giving financial wisdom.

## Simple Action Steps
- Decide on the type of financial gift that aligns with your family's needs.
- Consult your bank, brokerage, or financial advisor for setup.
- Pair the gift with a personal note, story, or even a symbolic keepsake.
- Share the "why" behind your gift so it feels personal, not transactional.

## Closing
This holiday, think beyond the fleeting joy of wrapping paper. By giving gifts that grow, you're offering something priceless—security, opportunity, and legacy.

When the toy is broken or the sweater outgrown, your financial gift will still be there—quietly building, quietly compounding, quietly saying, *"I invested in your future because I love you."*

The sweet spot is that these gifts don't have to stand alone. You can always wrap up your "financial future" present with a small, cost-conscious item that's given from the heart—a favorite book, a cozy blanket, or even a framed photo with your handwritten note tucked inside. The tangible gift delights in the moment, while the financial gift builds for the future. Together, they say, *"I cherish you today, and I believe in your tomorrow."*

**Cyndee Paulson-Heer**
Founder at Sass n' Soul
TheSassNSoulLife.com

# GIFTS THAT SPEAK THE HEART

By Cyndee Paulson-Heer

**Meaningful Ways to Celebrate the Men Who Matter**
It's easy to get caught up in the glitter and gift guides of the season—another tie, another gadget, another thing that ends up on a shelf. But the truth is, what most men cherish isn't another "item." Just like us gals—it's feeling seen, appreciated, and genuinely known.

Whether it's your partner, brother, father, or friend, the most memorable gifts are the ones that carry thought, time, and heart. They say, "*I know who you are.*" They bridge your shared history with the here and now—turning gratitude into something real, heartfelt, and lasting..

So this season, why not turn the **12 Days of Christmas** into something more meaningful? Instead of partridges and pear trees, give him twelve small gifts that tell your story, celebrate his passions, and show your love in action—one thoughtful surprise each day.

Here are twelve ideas to get you started and make this holiday season unforgettable:

**Gifts that speak louder than price tags.**
1. **Memory Jar of "Us"** - Fill a jar with handwritten memories, reasons why you love him, or a combination of both.
2. **Legacy Letter** - Write a heartfelt letter sharing how he's impacted your life; frame it or put it in a wax-sealed envelope.
3. **Custom Playlist or Vinyl Mix** - Tell your story through music—the soundtrack of "you two."
4. **Quality Time Coupon Book** - Experiences over things: a home-cooked meal, movie night, or a day off for him to just *be*.
5. **"Why I Admire You" Deck** - If you're feeling crafty—a deck of cards listing the traits you love most about him.
6. **Shared Journal** - A couple's journal to pass back and forth, capturing gratitude, goals, and dreams.
7. **Adventure Day** - Plan a day doing what he loves—fishing, hiking, live music, or exploring someplace new.
8. **Framed Lyric or Quote Print** - His favorite lyrics, poem, or an inside joke—framed with intention.

9. **Custom Map Art** - Highlight the places that tell your shared story: where you met, loved, and grew.

10. **Subscription That Fits His Passion** - Coffee, cigars, craft beer, books—choose what fuels him.

11. **A Handwritten "Future Memories" List** - Experiences you still want to create with him.

12. **A Day Off, Your Treat** - You take care of everything so he can rest and recharge.

At the heart of every meaningful gift is presence—the act of pausing long enough to ask, *What would make him feel loved, understood, and seen?* That's the magic that never fades.

**Cyndee Paulson-Heer**
Founder at Sass n' Soul
TheSassNSoulLife.com

# HAPPY HOLIDAYS FROM MY HOUSE TO YOURS

By Cyndee Paulson-Heer

As a teenager, I started playing Christmas music before Thanksgiving. It drove my family a little crazy, but for me, those familiar seasonal melodies lit the spark of the season — anticipation, magic, and the soft glow of hope.

The holidays meant decorating, noticing one another, laughing a little more, and letting kindness take the lead. Even the world outside our front door seemed gentler — strangers smiled more often, patience found its way into shoppers' hearts, and for a few precious weeks, a collective warmth seemed to wrap around everyone.

### Thanksgiving at Nana & Papa Choo-Choo's

The season always began at my dad's parents' home. Nana's pies had flaky crusts that felt like angels had rolled the dough themselves. Papa — who spent fifty years of his life on the railroad, earning the family nickname "Choo-Choo" — loved to "help" in the kitchen. When Nana wasn't looking, he'd adjust the temperatures on her burners. Nana would catch him out of the corner of her eyes and bark a sharp *"Dan!"* He'd retreat like a cartoon character fading into the wallpaper. We grandkids would bite our lips, trying not to giggle.

The food was unforgettable — perfectly moist turkey, buttery mashed potatoes, rich gravy — but it was the togetherness that made it sacred.

### Christmas at Nana & Papa Boat's

By Christmas week, we'd pack up and head to my mom's parents — Nana and Papa Boat — so named because they owned lakefront property and boats—and that's another story. Christmas was spent at their main house, which had a guest house, and that little cottage became my whole universe for one perfect week every year.

I adored my Papa Boat. His presence made everything feel larger than life. He was steady and kind with a playful, mischievously defiant edge that I am proud to say I unconsciously infused into my own character over the years.

We shared dinner in the pool room with the larger clan—then moved to the front house with my Aunt and first cousins for gift sharing. We gathered around the beautifully flocked white tree decorated only in red. Color wheels washed the room in shifting hues — pure magic to my young eyes.

Midnight meant linguica sandwiches — the sacred tradition of our Portuguese roots. Last year, as I stood over the stove, I told my husband, "This smell used to mean midnight." He smiled and asked, "What does it mean now?" I paused and softly answered, Family. "It will always mean: Family. Christmas. Tradition, and Love."

Some things never change — they just evolve.

### Christmas Day Rounds & Small Acts of Love

Christmas morning meant visiting a constellation of family homes — each smelling of cookies, pie, and a love language spoken through food. My great-grandmother, "Old Gramma," would give us simple gifts — a pair of socks or a hair ribbon wrapped in tissue. Gifts that fit her budget. I didn't understand why her gifts were so simple — why just socks or a clip when others gave gifts with "more substance"? But as I grew older, I came to see the beauty in her giving. Her gifts were given purely from love — not obligation, but from a soul who believed that giving, in any measure, was love.

### The Shifting of Time

But time, as it does, moved on. My grandparents are no longer with us, and the "rounds" have faded into memory. The table that once overflowed with pies and people now gathers fewer faces, and yes — our crusts are often store-bought. But love, I've learned, doesn't measure itself in perfect pastry. It measures in continuity — in the traditions that survive simply because we choose to carry them forward.

If you stop by my house on Christmas Eve, you'll still hear laughter amongst the same worn-out stories being told over and over. You'll still see cousins playing who only see each other a few times a year, and you'll still find a tray of linguica sandwiches — though we serve them around six instead of midnight. We open presents when the spirit moves us.

You'll see in-laws and family so tightly bonded that you might struggle to know who's who. That's how we like it — family by blood, by love, and by choice, all woven together in one big, joyful tangle.

### Connecting with Those Passed

When the laughter quiets and the dishes are drying, I steal away for a few moments. I slip into my favorite chair, light a candle, and put on Barbara Streisand's "Closer." As the music fills the room, I feel the veil between worlds disappear.

"So on this silent night
I call your name
And suddenly all time and space disappears.
I see your face in firelight,
I hold you close in memory,
And even though you're gone,
I know you're here . . ."

This is my small ritual of remembrance — a moment to connect with my mom, my dad, my grandparents, my brothers, and others who, though gone, still hold precious real estate in my heart. Sometimes I'll wink at one of them when something happens that I know they'd find funny or appreciate or simply just whisper, "I love you."

Their laughter still echoes through the walls of my world, and their spirit lives on in the way I love, host, and gather — in every candle lit, every meal shared, and every moment of connection that keeps them close.

### The Heart of the Season

Maybe the holidays are really a sacred act of re-membering — bringing the members of our stories—present and past—back together through food, music, and connecting in the magic of the present moment.

So, from my house to yours — may your holidays be filled with laughter that lingers, memories that warm the quiet corners, and the kind of magic that comes from simple acts of love.

This year, if the mood strikes, buy the person behind you in the Starbucks line a cup of coffee. Smile and say hello to a stranger. Send a handwritten note to someone you've lost touch with. These small gestures — these everyday acts of kindness — are the modern magic of the season, especially in an AI world where "personal touch" is fading.

**And now, dear reader, I ask — what rituals make your holidays memorable?**

# LAST-MINUTE GIFTS THAT STILL FEEL THOUGHTFUL

1. Locally roasted coffee + a cute mug
2. A handwritten "Top 5 Things I Adore About You" note
3. Cozy socks + a mini self-care quote card
4. A digital gift card to their favorite small biz
5. A journal and pen tied with ribbon (*instant reflection kit!*)
6. Hand-mixed spice jar labeled "*Soul Seasoning*"
7. Homemade cookies in a mason jar with a tag: "*Made with Sass & Soul*"
8. Spotify playlist: "Songs That Sound Like You"
9. Scented candle + a personal intention card
10. One hour of your time — coffee date, errand buddy, afternoon happy hour

**Cindy Louis**

# PRESENT VS PRESENTS

By Cindy Louis

The holiday season is upon us — *the countdown to Christmas … or maybe the countdown to anxiety.*

Think about it: when you hear, "Only 35 shopping days left until Christmas!" what happens in your body? A quickened heartbeat? A mental checklist that starts multiplying like snowflakes?

For many of us, panic sets in. We start our gift list, calculate our budget, try to remember what everyone gave us last year (if they did), and begin the annual cycle of stress. Even if you don't personally celebrate Christmas, the pressure can still sneak in. Maybe you want to acknowledge friends or family who do celebrate — and before you know it, you're swept up in the same consumer whirlwind.

Let's pause for a moment.
Take a deep breath.
And another.

That "countdown" isn't sacred — it's retail-driven. Stores want us to buy more things people don't really need, often with money we don't really have.

Now, look at your gift list (if you've started one) and ask yourself a few grounding questions:

- Where do my people live — nearby or out of state?
- Will I actually see them during the holidays?
- How often do I connect with them during the year?
- What's my true gift-giving budget?
- Most importantly — what do they mean to my life and my well-being?

Here's a truth worth holding onto: more than half of Americans feel lonely at Christmas. Even those who seem the busiest — the planners, decorators, and dinner hosts — can feel isolated in all the chaos. The frenzy of "doing it all" can mask a quiet ache underneath.

And even when you're surrounded by people, loneliness can still find you.

So we buy things. We overfill our schedules. We give to fill a void — but it rarely works.

What we really crave isn't more *stuff*. It's connection.

And connection takes *time* and it's the most meaningful gift of all.

**Try These Simple Sentences This Season:**

**For people you'll see:**
"This year, instead of bringing gifts, I'd love to bring a fun game for all of us to play."

**For people far away:**
"I really miss seeing you during the holidays. Can we schedule a video call to connect and reminisce?"

**For people you want to see but often don't:**
"Do you have time for a walk or lunch before Christmas? I'd love to catch up."

**For someone who might be lonely (but won't admit it):**
"Can I swing by this afternoon or tomorrow just to say hi?"

*(Last-minute invitations often work best — they can't talk themselves out of it!)*

**The Conversations That Matter:**
- Tell them how much you value their presence — and explain why you're focusing on *being present* this year instead of buying presents.
- Set a time limit if needed — respect their time and yours.
- Ask real questions and let them talk.
- Listen deeply — not just to reply, to understand.
- Make them feel wanted and appreciated.
- Tell them how they enrich your life — and why it matters.
- Reminisce about a fun or meaningful memory.
- Share laughter — even a couple of silly jokes will do.
- Before you part, schedule your *next* connection — a coffee date, call, or walk. Keep the thread alive.

**Need Some Holiday Humor? Try These:**
- Where does a polar bear keep his money?
- **In a snowbank.**

- What did the triangle say to the circle?
- **You're pointless.**

- What did the janitor say when he jumped out of the closet?

- **Supplies!**

- What do you call it when a snowman throws a tantrum?
- **A meltdown.**

- I ordered a chicken and an egg online — I'll let you know which comes first.

So, are you ready to toss the pressure of the countdown clock and reclaim your peace?

This year, free yourself from the frenzy. Slow down, breathe, and give the most valuable gift of all — You—Your time—**Your presence.**

## Kristy Rogers
### Business-Friends Philosophy

# SLEIGH IT YOUR WAY: A SELF-LOVED HOLIDAY SEASON

By Kristy Rogers

*"You can't get this wrong. **The goal is to honor where you are — this year.**"*

The holidays are coming—ready or not! But before the season sweeps you away, pause for a moment and ask yourself:
**"For *this* year, what do *I* need?"**

Hint: You always want to honor yourself first—not in a selfish way. In a way that "puts the mask on you," before you take care of others.

When you think about the holidays approaching, what comes to mind?

Are you:
- Excited?
- Ready to decorate this very moment?
- Dreading it?
- Not caring much at all?
- Planning to just do the same routine as always?

Whatever your answer, accept it. Be okay with it. It's *your truth*—at least for now. Be honest. You can't get this wrong. The goal is to honor where you are—*this year*.

### The Year Everything Changed
Several years ago, I had had it. Another holiday season of "same old, same old."

Thanksgiving meant the same food, same routine, same bore-fest. Christmas was anticlimactic, lonely, and honestly, a bit depressing. New Year's Eve? Uneventful.

My holidays looked nothing like the Hallmark movies I secretly adore.

Then it hit me—**I can redefine what the holidays mean to me.** My experience starts with my thoughts, and I can change those.

I asked myself, "For this year, what do I want to experience? How do I want it to go?"

That's when everything shifted.
- I took myself to **Afternoon Tea the day before Thanksgiving**—and it was magical.
- On Christmas, I surprised my family with **Christmas Bingo**, bringing laughter, playfulness, and joy.
- For New Year's Eve, I invited four single girlfriends over for **Japanese takeout and ice cream sundaes**.

That was the year my relationship with the holidays transformed. Now, I actually *look forward* to them—because they reflect *me*, right where I am in life.

## Your Turn: For THIS YEAR
Ask yourself:
- What do you want to experience?
- How do you want each holiday to feel?

Let's start with emotions. What good-feeling emotions do you want to experience this year?

Many of us default to stress, dread, or obligation because all we can think about is the workload, the same worn-out routines, the cost, or the past imbalance.

**Reality check:** the people you celebrate with may be feeling the same way.

Are you ready for a change?

What if this year felt more...
- Connected
- Joyful
- Supported
- Spacious
- Fun
- Fresh
- Delightful

Wouldn't that bring you more joy?

Now, ask yourself: **What will give me those feelings?**

## Focus on Just This Year
You don't have to overhaul everything forever—just focus on *this year*.

Ask yourself:
- What do I want more of?
- What do I want less of?
- What can I simplify?
- What have I always wanted to try?
- What's something new I can add?
- What brings me fun and joy?

When you make *this year* good for yourself, it positively affects everyone around you.

You might even invite your family or friends to answer these same questions—who knows what new ideas or traditions might spark?

## If This Year Feels Uninspired
If you're going through a tough time, give yourself a break. Your emotions are valid. Maybe this year isn't about celebrating. Maybe it's about simply getting through peacefully and gently.

Honor that.

A couple of years ago, I didn't decorate, didn't host, and didn't "do" the holidays. I just let it be. And looking back, that choice was beautiful—it honored where I truly was at that point in time.

## Reimagining the Celebration
When you're ready to re-engage, look at each aspect of the holidays through your *This Year* lens:
- Food & beverages
- Cooking
- Decorating (indoors, outdoors, and table)
- Gifts & shopping
- Clean up
- People
- Location
- Timing

Which parts feel the most draining? Tune in to your emotions. Listening can be an invitation for change. The goal: create **joyful feelings**—*this year*.

## Ideas to Get You Started
- Try new **hot chocolate recipes** until you find your favorite. (Here's mine: Bon Appétit's Best Hot Chocolate)
- Attend a **local holiday concert or event**. I once took a pedi-cab ride through a neighborhood of dazzling lights—pure fun! Check Eventbrite or search "holiday events near me."
- Host **brunch or lunch** instead of dinner.
- Change up your **menu**—just because you always make turkey doesn't mean you can't change it up this year.
- Make **decorating** a joy, not a chore—focus on how good it feels when it's done, and if the mood strikes, invite some friends over for a decorating party.
- **Decorate early** so you can enjoy it longer.
- Use **festive paper plates** (TJ Maxx has great ones!).

- Try **new recipes** or **theme nights**.
- Declare a **no-gift holiday** (except for kids).
- Do a **stockings-only** exchange.
- Give **consumable or handmade gifts**.
- Share the **workload**—invite help with cooking and cleanup.

Looking at the holidays from the *This Year* perspective creates space to meet you right where you are, express creativity, and rediscover the magic that feels good to you.

### If You're Celebrating Solo

For those of us who live alone, the shift from a lively gathering to the sudden quiet of an empty house can feel jarring. I know that feeling well—Christmas brunch ends, everyone leaves, and suddenly the house is still. **Plan ahead for that moment.** Make yourself a special dinner or plan an activity you love—something that fills your heart.

### My Wish For you

May *this year* be your most empowering, soul-nourishing holiday season yet.

Celebrate in a way that honors **you first**—and watch how joy naturally follows.

**Cheers to you and your beautiful, authentic holidays!**

*About Kristy: Building better relationships starts with understanding. The Business-Friends Philosophy offers a new perspective that makes connecting — in business and life — so much easier*

### Connect With Kristy

www.linkedin.com/in/kristyrogersconnects
Info@KristyRogersConnects.com

# SIMPLE JOYS TO ADD A SPARK TO YOUR SEASON

1. Light candles at dinner — even if it's takeout
2. Put on your favorite childhood holiday songs
3. Write one thank-you note, each week, from Thanksgiving till Christmas
4. Watch the lights with cocoa, family, and/or friends instead of scrolling
5. Beautifully wrap a handful of gifts — think, before Christmas, gift bags were a thing
6. Take a midnight walk under twinkle lights with someone you love
7. Donate a toy or meal anonymously
8. Make snow (or glitter) angels
9. Drink from your prettiest glass, and favorite Holiday mugs
10. Say "I love you" more than usual

**Cyndee Paulson-Heer**
Founder at Sass n' Soul
TheSassNSoulLife.com

# CUT FROM A DIFFERENT CLOTH: THE SARA BLAKELY STORY

By Cyndee Paulson-Heer

*How one woman's refusal to play small reshaped an industry—and inspired a generation to think bigger.*

She didn't invent shapewear.
She reinvented self-belief.

One humid Florida morning in 1998, Sara Blakely stood in front of her mirror, scissors in hand, staring down a pair of control-top pantyhose. She wanted smoother lines under white pants—not a revolutionary product. But with one decisive snip, she didn't just cut off the feet; she cut through limitation. What started as a personal fix would soon transform into a billion-dollar empire and an enduring symbol of what happens when women trust their intuition and act on it.

### The Humble Hustle

Sara didn't start her story in a boardroom or a branding meeting. She started in the trenches—selling fax machines door-to-door under the sweltering Florida sun, facing rejection on repeat. She failed the LSAT twice. She knew what "no" sounded like, felt like, and how heavy it could sit in your bones.

But she also knew that "no" wasn't a stop sign. It was an invitation to pivot.

Her father often asked at the dinner table, *"What did you fail at today?"* Failure wasn't shameful in her house—it was expected, even celebrated. That reframe became her greatest asset. Instead of avoiding mistakes, she collected them like merit badges on her way to mastery.

*"Failure is nothing more than life's way of nudging you in a better direction."* – Sara Blakely

It was in that spirit of experimentation that she took her $5,000 in savings, a roll of pantyhose, and an unstoppable sense of humor—and began creating something no one else could see yet.

### The $5,000 Leap

Sara had no fashion degree, no investor, no business plan—just an unshakable belief that women deserved better. She called dozens of hosiery mills, only to hear the same answer: *Not interested.*

Until one day, one owner—thanks to his daughters—said yes. That yes cracked open a door, and she sprinted through it.

She wrote her own patent, created her first packaging design, and drove store to store convincing buyers to give her product a chance. Her big break came when she personally demonstrated her prototype to a Neiman Marcus buyer—literally in a dressing room.

Weeks later, *Oprah* named *Spanx* her favorite product of the year.

Sara's phone rang off the hook, her apartment became a shipping center, and her life changed forever.

But what stands out most isn't how she succeeded—it's how she stayed *herself* in the process.

### Authenticity in Action
While other companies led with perfection, Sara led with personality. She laughed in her marketing videos, cracked jokes on stage, and built a brand around *real women* with *real bodies*. She didn't pretend to be something she wasn't—she embodied everything she was.

She didn't outsource her soul.

Even as Spanx scaled into the billions, she stayed deeply human. When she sold a majority stake of the company in 2021, she gave each of her employees $10,000 in cash and two first-class plane tickets to anywhere in the world—a literal manifestation of her mantra: *When you rise, bring others with you.*

"It's not about the what. It's about the why—and the joy you bring to the journey."

### Legacy in Motion
Sara Blakely could have stopped at billionaire. Instead, she became a benefactor.

Through the Sara Blakely Foundation, she's funded scholarships for young women, supported female entrepreneurs, and joined the *Giving Pledge* to donate half her wealth to causes that lift others. Her message has remained the same for over two decades:
Empower women to believe in their ideas, bet on themselves, and bring their boldest selves to the table.

*"Failure is nothing more than life's way of nudging you in a better direction."*

Her legacy isn't just stretchy fabric—it's a flexible mindset that invites women everywhere to expand what they believe is possible.

"The world doesn't need another Spanx. It needs more women who believe in themselves."

### Soul Reflection: What She Teaches Us
Sara's journey is a masterclass in authenticity, grit, and grace. She didn't wait for permission. She didn't wait for perfect timing. She trusted that the very thing that annoyed her—the everyday discomfort of pantyhose—might be the divine whisper of purpose calling her forward.

Innovation doesn't always roar. Sometimes it giggles in a dressing room mirror.

Her story is a reminder that greatness rarely arrives dressed for the occasion. It often shows up barefoot, holding scissors, and saying, "Let's give this a go."

Sara's story is a perfect example of:
Self-trust
Acting on intuition
Resilience
Contribution
Leading with purpose
And living every single day, as though you are legend . . . and, Sara Blakey IS def Legend!

### Journaling Prompt
*What frustration or idea have you brushed aside that might actually be your next big breakthrough?*

### Sassy & Soulful Takeaway
You don't need investors to invest in yourself.

All you need is courage, curiosity, and a pair of metaphorical scissors.

# THE ANATOMY OF GRIT

Grit: Courage and resolve; Strength of character

## Character - The sum total of who you are at your core

Character is the inner framework that holds you upright when life tilts sideways. It is authenticity in action — the choice to remain aligned with your values, even when pressure tries to reshape you.

Character is not about perfection; it is about principle. It is the part of you that stays when applause fades, when the crowd leaves, and when no one is watching.

**Sass n' Soul Truth:**
Character is your soul's signature.

## Resolve - The determination to go the distance

Resolve is the deep, unshakable "I will find a way." It is the devotion behind daily action and the courage to begin again when the path gets messy. Resolve is the steady energy that transforms intention into impact, turning your "why" into a life well-lived.

**Sass n' Soul Truth:**
Resolve is fire with direction.

## Resilience - The spirit of never giving up

Resilience is how you rise, recalibrate, and return. It turns setbacks into recalibration and realignment instead of defeat. It keeps you flexible when life bends you, grounded when life "tests" you.

**Sass n' Soul Truth:**
You may bend. You may break! But you will rise again.

## Courage - Strength to act in the face of fear

Courage is the willingness to begin before you feel ready. It's standing graciously in your truth and stepping forward while your knees still shake. Courage is the ignition point of every gritty woman's journey.

**Sass n' Soul Truth:**
Bold moves birth beautiful legacies.

## Passion - The Fire of Purpose

Passion fuels consistency. It's the force that pulls you forward when motivation fades. Passion makes the long game meaningful and the work soulful.

**Sass n' Soul Truth:**
Your why is your lighthouse.

## Discipline - The will to get 'er done

Discipline is resolve in motion. It's the quiet daily practice that transforms desire into mastery. Not about hustle — about honoring your commitment to yourself.

**Sass n' Soul Truth:**
Devotion over motivation.

## Integrity - The Compass of Alignment

Integrity keeps your grit clean, conscious, and heart-led. It ensures you don't lose yourself while chasing the dream. It is the alignment between your soul, values, and actions.

**Sass n' Soul truth:**
Hold your truth when the world wobbles.

## Contribution - The spirit of giving back

The highest expression of grit expands beyond self.
When you've built strength, you lift others.
When you've found your voice, you share it.
When you've made your mark, you help others make theirs.

**Sass n' Soul Truth:**
Lift as you rise.

## Grit = Character + Courage + Compassion + Contribution

The alchemy of showing up, staying true, and standing tall — with humor, heart, and humanity intact.

# COZY RITUALS FOR THE SOUL

1. Light a candle and reflect on your year
2. Journal about three things you're proud of
3. Take a long, hot bath with your favorite bath bomb, candles, and your favorite Holiday playlist
4. Sip tea from your favorite holiday mug while watching the sunrise
5. Diffuse your favorite essential oils and journal about your favorite moments from the day.
6. Declutter one drawer — make space for new energy
7. Write a letter to your future self
8. Go tech-free for one evening
9. Read something uplifting before bed
10. Sleep in without guilt

**Elizabeth Clarke**
Owner/President of Structure Groups

# UNWRAPPING YOUR OWN POWER: A HOLIDAY REFLECTION

By Elizabeth Clarke

The holidays have a way of reminding us how much we pour into everyone else, our families, our teams, our communities. But somewhere between the shopping lists and social calendars, it's easy to forget ourselves.

This season, I want to challenge every woman reading this to unwrap something truly powerful....YOU!

Take a quiet moment, away from the noise and glitter, to reflect on what you've accomplished this year, not just the milestones, but the moments you showed up when it would've been easier not to. The times you stayed kind, stayed strong, or simply stayed present.

Empowerment doesn't always roar. Sometimes, it whispers, "You're doing enough."

So as we close out the year, let's celebrate progress over perfection, courage over control, and connection over chaos. Surround yourself with people who fill your cup. And, remember, you've already given the world one of its greatest gifts: a woman who leads with heart.

# HEARTFELT WAYS TO GIVE BACK

1. Pay for someone's coffee behind you in line
2. Drop handwritten notes of encouragement in random places—where they will be seen. I dropped them at Barnes and Noble, one year.
3. Volunteer an hour — not a day — at a local cause
4. Tip double, to that deserving person, once this month
5. Buy extra gloves or scarves to hand out
6. Give a food gift card to a homeless person . . . or a coffee card to a stranger
7. Compliment strangers, at least once each day
8. Leave a thank-you note for a delivery driver
9. Gift wrap donations for a women's shelter
10. Forgive someone quietly — the frequency will carry

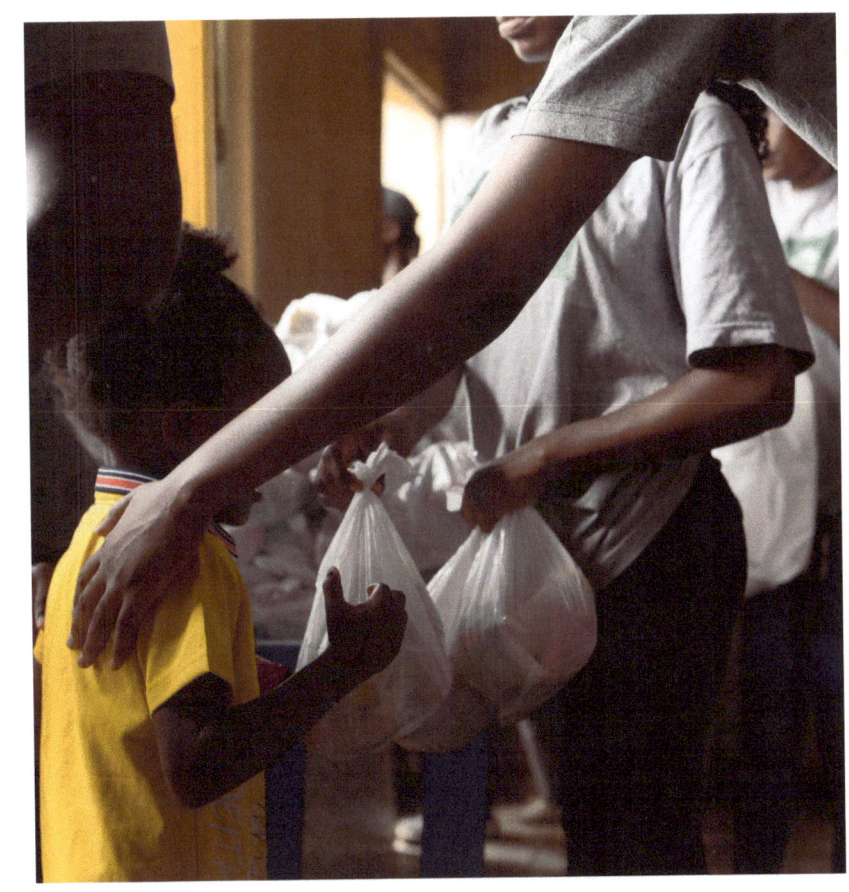

# ELEANOR ROOSEVELT: A LIFE OF COURAGE, COMPASSION, AND CONSCIENCE

**Berenice Stephens**

By Berenice Stephens

---

*"Do what you feel in your heart to be right—for you'll be criticized anyway."*

Some lives remind us that greatness isn't bestowed by title or privilege but forged in the quiet conviction to do what is right—again and again—especially when it's hard. Eleanor Roosevelt lived such a life. She redefined what it meant to lead, to serve, and to be a woman of substance in a world that expected her to stand invisibly in her husband's shadow and stay silent.

### Courage in the Face of Convention
As First Lady, she was expected to smile, entertain, and fade into the background of history. Instead, she took the podium. She wrote daily columns, traveled to war zones, met with coal miners and soldiers, and listened to those whose voices went unheard. She turned fear into fuel, proving that courage is not the absence of doubt but the decision to move forward anyway.

> *"Courage isn't the absence of doubt—it's the decision to move forward anyway."*

### Authenticity in Action
Roosevelt's moral compass never wavered toward popularity. She spoke truth when it was unpopular, advocated for racial equality when it was dangerous, and insisted that human dignity was not negotiable. Her words carried weight because her life embodied them. Integrity, for her, was not a performance—it was a practice.

### Transforming Privilege into Purpose
Born into privilege, she could have lived a comfortable life of smiles, waves, and appearances. Instead, she transformed her position into a platform. Her influence wasn't loud; it was lasting. As Chair of the United Nations Commission on Human Rights, she shepherded the creation of the Universal Declaration of Human Rights—an achievement that continues to shape the moral fabric of nations today.

### The Spirit of the Season
The holiday season invites us to slow down—to step out of the whirlwind of doing and into the quiet of being. It calls us to look beyond what we've accumulated and reflect instead on what we've contributed—the relationships we've nurtured, the moments we've shared, and the lives we've touched.

Eleanor Roosevelt's legacy reminds us of what truly matters—the courage to act on conscience, the humility to serve others, and the strength to lead with love. She didn't just speak of a better world—she rolled up her sleeves and helped build it.

In a time when uncertainty is rippling through every corner of our culture, we are reminded to soften—to see the humanity in one another and remember what unites us. Real legacy is woven from compassion, not consumerism. From collaboration, not competition. From connection, not division. Eleanor Roosevelt embodied these truths year-round. Her generosity wasn't wrapped in ribbons or reserved for December; it was stitched into the fabric of her everyday choices.

She believed that kindness was a form of courage, that service was love in motion, and that each of us carries the power to make the world a little fairer, a little kinder, a little more awake. Her life whispers to us even now—Do good quietly. Love fiercely. Let your convictions outshine the ornaments.

As the lights twinkle across our homes and hearts, may we follow her lead—choosing meaning over noise, empathy over ego, and understanding over judgement. The spirit of the season ought not be about doing more; it ought be about being more—more open, more compassionate, more aligned with the collective truth that love beats all hearts, no matter the culture or ethnicity, and at the core we are each other's keepers.

Roosevelt didn't wait for an invitation to make a difference, and neither should we. Whether through a handwritten note, a small act of generosity, or the courage to stand for what's right, each of us holds the potential to embody the holiday spirit in its highest form: love made visible.

Perhaps this year, we take it one step further—in the name of love. Buy a cup of coffee for the stranger behind you in line. Leave a kind note on a windshield. Compliment someone without reason. These seemingly small gestures carry extraordinary power: they ripple outward, reminding others that goodness still lives among us.

Love is the thread that runs through every faith and philosophy.

> *"She didn't wait for an invitation to make a difference —and neither should we."*

If we focused on those shared qualities—rather than the labels that divide us—we'd discover what truly matters: love, compassion, kindness, and our shared humanity.

So, as one year folds gently into the next, may we carry Eleanor Roosevelt's example forward—quietly, courageously, and with hearts wide open. For that is how one life can touch another, and we can reunite under the banner of love and community.

**Reflect & Renew**

- When have I done the thing I thought I could not do?
- Where am I still waiting for permission to act on what I know is right?
- If leadership is moral courage in motion, what legacy will I begin building today?

*This season, may your kindness be your signature—and your love, your legacy.*

Berenice Stephens is an activist who stands for equality, fairness, and peace.

# SWEET & SIMPLE TREATS TO WHIP UP

1. Peppermint bark in 15 minutes—see recipe below
2. Cocoa bar with toppings (peppermint, cayenne, cinnamon, marshmallows, shaved chocolate)
3. "Reindeer mix" trail snack in mason jars
4. Baked brie with honey & cranberries
5. Holiday popcorn (white chocolate + sprinkles)
6. Sugared cranberries for cocktails
7. Homemade vanilla sugar
8. Soul-fire martinis
9. Mini pancake stacks with powdered sugar snow
10. Festive fruit skewers with marshmallow dip

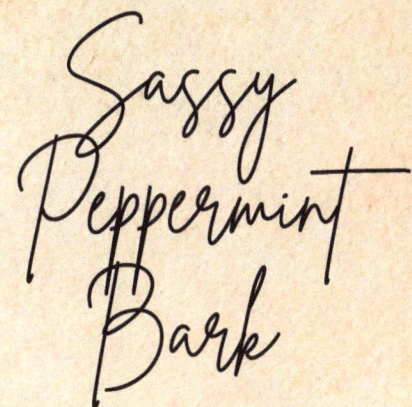

# Sassy Peppermint Bark

**Makes:** About 1 ½ pounds
**Prep time:** 15 minutes + cooling

## Ingredients:

- **12 oz semisweet or dark chocolate chips** (or chopped bar chocolate)
- **12 oz white chocolate chips** (or chopped bar chocolate)
- **½ tsp peppermint extract** (optional but amazing)
- **½ cup crushed candy canes or peppermint candies**
- **1 tsp coconut oil** (optional, for smoother melting)

## Directions:

**Prep it.**
- Line a baking sheet with parchment paper or wax paper.

**Melt the dark layer.**
- In a heatproof bowl, melt dark chocolate in the microwave (30-second intervals, stirring each time) until smooth.
- Stir in half the peppermint extract (if using) and a touch of coconut oil for gloss.

**Spread & chill.**
- Pour onto the prepared pan, spreading evenly to about ¼ inch thick.
- Chill in the fridge for 10-15 minutes until firm but not rock solid.

**Melt the white chocolate.**
- Repeat the process with the white chocolate, adding the remaining peppermint extract.

**Top & swirl.**
- Pour the white layer over the dark chocolate. Gently spread, then sprinkle crushed candy canes evenly over the top.
- For a pretty marble look, drag a skewer lightly through the top layer before it sets.

**Set & snap.**
- Chill for 20-30 minutes until completely firm. Break into rustic pieces or cut into clean squares.

Wrap in cellophane bags tied with ribbon and a tag that says: *"Handcrafted with love, sass, especially for you."*

Or layer pieces in a mason jar with tissue paper for a quick, gorgeous hostess gift. Finish off the neck with a festive ribbon.

**Cyndee Paulson-Heer**
Founder at Sass n' Soul
TheSassNSoulLife.com

# CLOSING THE CHAPTER: A YEAR-END REFLECTION

By Cyndee Paulson-Heer

As the year draws to a close, the pages of our lives fill with memories—some triumphant, some tender, and others quietly transformative. The end of the year isn't just a time for resolutions; it's an invitation to pause, reflect, and realign with who you've become and where your soul longs to go next.

Journaling is one of the most powerful ways to bridge the space between who you were and who you are becoming. It captures the whispers of gratitude, the lessons of growth, and the dreams waiting just beyond the horizon. When you take time to reflect, you give meaning to the moments that shaped you—and create intention for the ones ahead.

This year, instead of rushing into "what's next," gift yourself a little time with your thoughts. Light a candle, pour something warm or sparkling, and write freely. Let your heart speak without judgment or agenda. As you answer the prompts below, you may rediscover forgotten victories, release lingering doubts, and rekindle your sense of purpose.

*Endings aren't endings at all—they're simply the quiet breath, the gentle pause, before a beautiful new beginning.*

**31 End-of-Year Journaling Prompts—one for each day in December**
*Reflect. Release. Realign. Rekindle your magic as you prepare to step into a brand-new year.*

**Reflect**
- What word best captures the essence of this past year for you—and why?
- What surprised you most about yourself this year?
- What challenge helped you grow the most?
- What did you let go of that made space for something better?
- What moment are you most proud of—and what did it teach you?
- Where did you hold yourself back, and why?
- What old story did you finally rewrite?
- Who showed up for you this year in unexpected ways?
- What did you rediscover about your own strength, creativity, or spirit?

- What became less important than you once thought it was?

## Release & Gratitude
- List five things that made your soul smile this year.
- What personal victory deserves a celebration—no matter how small?
- What lesson are you most grateful for (even if it came wrapped in difficulty)?
- How have your priorities shifted in the past twelve months?
- What did you say "yes" to that expanded your life?
- What did you say "no" to that protected your peace?
- Who or what helped you feel most like *yourself* this year?

## Realign & Renew
- What energy or intention do you want to carry into the new year?
- What word, phrase, or mantra will guide your next chapter?
- How do you want to feel at the end of next year?
- What's one habit, mindset, or belief you're ready to release?
- What dream is quietly asking for your attention?
- What legacy do you want to continue building in the coming year?
- If next year were your most aligned, authentic year yet—what would it look like?

## Rekindle Your Sass & Soul
- What did your "Sassy Self" teach your "Serious Self" this year?
- When did you feel most soulful, grounded, or alive?
- What moment this year made you say, "This is *me* living my truth"?
- How will you celebrate yourself before this year closes?
- What's one bold, beautiful way you can start the new year with intention?
- How will you make next year the one where you Live as *Though You Are Legend*?

## Love
- What did this year teach you about love—

love for yourself, for others, and for life itself?

## In Closing
As this year gently comes to a close, take a moment to honor how far you've come. The lessons, the laughter, the tears, and the quiet moments of courage—all of it has helped shape the woman you are right now. Let this month of journaling remind you that endings are not finales—they're invitations. Step into the new year grounded in gratitude, guided by intention, and glowing with the wisdom only lived experience can give. You've evolved, you've risen, and now it's time to write your next chapter—one filled with purpose, joy, and that unmistakable spark of Sass n' Soul.

# BUDGET-FRIENDLY GIFTS WITH BIG HEART

1. **"Open When…" Letters** – Write a handful of envelopes labeled "Open when you're sad," "Open when you need courage," "Open when you forget how amazing you are." Fill them with personal notes, quotes, or affirmations.

2. **Legacy Recipe Card** – Handwrite a favorite family recipe, add a memory about it, and tie it with twine to a small whisk or wooden spoon.

3. **Personalized Candle Label** – Buy a simple candle and relabel it with something meaningful like "Calm in Chaos," "Courage & Cocoa," or "Soul-fire Energy."

4. **"Sass in a Jar"** – Fill a mason jar with confidence quotes, compliments, or affirmations. Label: "One for every time you forget your sparkle."

5. **Memory Ornament** – Use a clear ornament and fill it with tiny notes, glitter, or dried flowers symbolizing your friendship or shared moments.

6. **The Gratitude Chain** – Cut strips of paper and write one thing you appreciate about the person on each. Loop and tape into a paper chain. They can add to it all year.

7. **Soul Playlist** – Create a playlist of songs that remind you of their strength, joy, or journey – title it "Your Legendary Soundtrack."

8. **Framed Quote Collage** – Print or handwrite a handful of quotes that reflect who they are. Frame them in a thrifted or repainted frame for a chic, personal touch.

9. **The 12 Days of You** – 12 small envelopes or notes, each revealing a reason you love or appreciate them – one to open each day.

10. **Quality Time Coupon** – Give the gift of your time

   - *One Movie Night – You Pick the Flick & the Snacks*
   - *Coffee & Conversation – No Phones, Just Us*
   - *Afternoon Adventure – Walk, Picnic, or Wander*
   - *Creative Playdate – Paint, Craft, or Bake Together*
   - *Your Playlist, My Company – A Night of Music & Memories*
   - *Dog Walk & Talk – Fresh Air, Good Vibes, No Agenda*
   - *Story Swap – You tell yours, I'll tell mine, and I'll really listen*
   - *Helper Hour – One hour of my time as your helper*

# QUICK DÉCOR THAT DELIVERS INSTANT CHEER

1. Wrap fairy lights around your favorite mirror
2. Fill a bowl with ornaments — centerpiece, done
3. Tie ribbon around doorknobs—holiday spirit added
4. Stack wrapped boxes for holiday decorations— no bows
5. Add cinnamon sticks or dried orange slices to candles—ahh, the scents of the season
6. Frame your favorite quote of the season—hang it somewhere where you will often see it
7. Make snowflakes—hang them from the ceiling with fishing line
8. Use gift tags as ornaments
9. Decorate your work area—pause to appreciate the season
10. Display past holiday cards as wall art—family and friends love seeing that you cared enough to keep their snail-mail love
11. Wrap your front door like a gift — wide ribbon, big bow. You get the picture

12. Cluster candles of different heights on a tray with pinecones or ornaments
13. Fill clear vases with cranberries or peppermint candies and add a white candle
14. Hang ornaments from a chandelier or light fixture
15. Drape garland or lights around a mirror or headboard — soft, ambient glow in minutes
16. Place sprigs of evergreen or eucalyptus in unexpected spots—bathroom, entryway, kitchen window
17. Swap out your throw pillows or blankets for something cozy and seasonal — faux fur, plaid, or velvet
18. Use metallic spray paint on pinecones or branches for instant glam
19. Tie small bells or charms on wine glasses for a festive touch during gatherings
20. Hang a single ornament from your rearview mirror or workspace — a tiny reminder of the magic season

# FROM MY HEART TO YOURS

**Cyndee Paulson-Heer**
Founder at Sass n' Soul
TheSassNSoulLife.com

By Cyndee Paulson-Heer

When my brother Dave was alive, every Christmas Eve we'd take our annual stroll down *Cocktail Lane*. What began as a playful experiment—me mixing two or three new creations for him to try—soon became a most treasured tradition. He'd sip, savor, and cast his vote with that familiar twinkle in his eye, declaring the winner of the night. Now, he lives on as I carry that ritual forward with my youngest son—our glasses filled with cocktails, and an occasional spiked cocoa, and our hearts steeped in memory, mischief, and endless buckets of love.

# Soul-fire Martini

—a recipe from the kitchen of Cyndee Paulson-Heer

**Flavor Mood:** Think molten chocolate meets espresso fire — silky, spiced, and a little seductive. This isn't your average holiday cocktail; it's a love letter with a kick.

## Ingredients:

**(makes 2 martinis)**

- **2 oz** Kahlúa Espresso (or Kahlúa Original + a splash of cold espresso)
- **1½ oz** vodka (*vanilla or chocolate vodka works beautifully*)
- **½ oz** Fireball Cinnamon Whiskey (*for that signature heat*)
- **1 oz** dark crème de cacao (*rich chocolate depth*)
- **½ oz** maple syrup or simple syrup (*to smooth the spice*)
- **⅛ tsp** cayenne pepper (*trust the process*)
- **Pinch** of cinnamon
- **Pinch** of pink Himalayan salt
- **1 generous scoop of Love** (Worry not — this invisible ingredient fits in any glass. It adds depth, not volume.)

**Garnish & Rim**
- Cocoa powder + cinnamon sugar mix for the rim
- Mini dark chocolate square or chili pepper slice for garnish
- Optional: A drizzle of chocolate syrup in the glass before pouring

*Whipped Soul Topping—optional*
- **½ cup** heavy whipping cream
- **1 tsp** maple syrup
- **¼ tsp** vanilla
- **Dusting:** cocoa + cinnamon — feel free to add a little love dust—there's no such thing as too much love.

## Directions:

**Prep the Glasses:**
- Run a bit of maple syrup or chocolate syrup around the rim of each martini glass. Dip in the cocoa-cinnamon mix. Set aside in the freezer to chill.

**Shake Up the Soul:**
- In a cocktail shaker filled with ice, add Kahlúa, vodka, Fireball, crème de cacao, maple syrup, cayenne, cinnamon, salt, and your *Endless Buckets of Love.*

**Shake It Like You Mean It:**
- Shake vigorously — the goal is a frosty shaker and a perfectly blended, velvety pour.

**Pour & Present:**
- Strain into your chilled martini glasses. Garnish with a dark chocolate square, a light dusting of cinnamon, or a delicate red chili slice for that dramatic flair.

**Elizabeth Clarke**
Owner/President of Structure Groups

# BECOMING LEGENDARY

By Elizabeth Clarke

There's a moment usually somewhere between your second cup of coffee and your third life crisis... when you realize that "finding yourself" isn't about discovering something new. It's about remembering who you were before the world told you who to be.

We spend years chasing the next title, paycheck, or version of success that looks good on paper. We measure our worth in metrics, likes, and other people's opinions and somewhere along the way, we start losing sight of our own reflection. But real confidence? Real peace? It begins the moment you stop auditioning for your own life.

Authenticity isn't just a buzzword. It's rebellion in heels (or sneakers, or barefoot on your paddleboard). It's the quiet but powerful act of showing up as yourself...unfiltered, unbothered, and unapologetically human. It's saying, "I'm done shrinking to make others comfortable."

Here's the secret no one tells you: legends aren't born out of perfection. They rise from the mess, the late nights, the risks, the moments you question everything and keep going anyway. Being legendary isn't about fame or recognition. It's about presence, being fully awake to your own life.

It's waking up and choosing to live boldly, laugh loudly, love deeply, and lead with heart.

When you live like that, something shifts. People feel it. You stop chasing validation because you realize you already have everything you need. For me, that's grit, grace, and a story worth telling.

So, here's your reminder, darling: You don't become legendary by being flawless. You become legendary by being *real*. By being the woman who shows up, even when it's hard. The one who lifts others as she climbs. The one who's not afraid to take up space—to speak her truth, share her gifts, and fill the room with her presence—and to make it beautiful with her authenticity, grace, and light. Because when you choose authenticity over approval, your life becomes the greatest story ever told—and it's all yours.

*Elizabeth Clarke, a Discovery Bay resident since 1995, is President of the Discovery Bay Chamber of Commerce, where she builds partnerships and launched a Women's Leadership Panel spotlighting local businesswomen. She is also the Immediate Past President of the Byron Delta Lions Club, leading service projects like student vision screenings.*

As Owner and President of Structure Groups, a civil engineering firm, Elizabeth contributes to statewide industry boards. Recognized in **Fortune**, **Entrepreneur, and 110° Magazine**, she's celebrated for her blend of professional excellence, community service, and servant leadership—balancing purpose, passion, and impact in all she does.

*"Real confidence begins the moment you stop auditioning for your own life."*

**Susie Unruh, RDN**

# MINDFUL MEAL TIMING: A SIMPLE GUIDE TO SMARTER EATING

By Susie Unruh, RDN

### Time Rules
Time to get up, go to work, go to a meeting, do Pilates, take the kids to baseball, do laundry—the list never ends! It's "like living" in a psychedelic cartoon with calendars, clocks, alarm clocks, planners, cell phones, tablets—all beeping, ringing, and swirling around your head.

But when is it time to feed your brain and body?

Although the seemingly old-fashioned notion of set mealtimes can be challenging, it actually has scientific validity. There are ways to modify mealtime schedules that can improve your health, energy, and mood! Taking and making time to eat —even a snack—can be a challenge when you have a busy schedule and demands from others. If you've struggled with losing or maintaining weight, poor meal timing could be part of the problem.

### The Case for Timely Eating
It's virtually impossible for most busy adults to eat at 8:00 am, noon, and 5:00 pm every day. So why are those times beneficial? The key isn't the exact time on the clock—it's the timing.

There are two core principles that can help you manage meal timing and reap the health benefits:

1. No Skipping Meals.
2. No Long Gaps Between Meals.

### Principle 1: No Skipping Meals
A little "something" is usually better than "nothing" when it comes to meals. On especially busy days, you may have to string together a few small snacks to provide nourishment and energy.

Some simple math illustrates the importance of avoiding skipped meals:
- The average daily calorie intake for many women is 1,500-1,800 calories.
- If you're consuming 1,500 calories a day, dividing evenly means each meal should be about 500 calories.

If you skip breakfast, you're already 500 calories behind. Then, if you have a light lunch—say 300 calories—you're now 700 calories behind. What happens next? You're likely to eat those 700 calories later in the day, meaning you'll consume two-thirds of your daily calories in the last third of your day.

As your body doesn't efficiently burn those calories late in the day, years of this habit can result in gradual weight gain.

### Principle 2: No Long Gaps Between Meals

This principle complements the first. Ideally, you shouldn't go longer than 4-5 hours between meals. If necessary, have a small snack to fill the gap.

Understanding how foods affect hunger and energy levels can help you plan your meals and snacks.

### Understanding Food Metabolism

Foods are made up of carbohydrates, protein, and fat which are metabolized at different speeds:

### Carbohydrates

- Simple carbs (e.g., fruits, juices, sugars): Provide quick energy for 30 minutes to 1 hour.
- Complex carbs (e.g., bread, cereals, rice, pasta, potatoes): Provide energy for 2-3 hours.

### Protein

- Found in meats, beans, dairy, nuts, and seeds.
- Provides energy for 3-4 hours.

### Fat

- Found in oils, butter, margarine, mayo, salad dressings, and fried foods.
- Takes the longest to digest, providing energy for 6-8 hours.

Aim to include a good source of protein, complex carbohydrates, and healthy fats (vegetable-based) at each meal.

Taking control of your meal timing doesn't have to feel like another overwhelming task on your to-do list. By following the simple principles of No Skipping and No Long Gaps, you can create a routine that supports your energy, mood, and overall health. Remember, it's not about perfection—it's about making small, consistent changes that align with your lifestyle. Start today, and let mindful meal timing be your first step toward a healthier, more balanced you.

*"Healthy eating isn't just about food; it's about creating a rhythm that fuels your body and mind throughout the day."*

A NEW CHAPTER BEGINS

# FENIX TV

## IS NOW ON YOUTUBE

TUNE IN FOR THE SAME INSPIRING CONTENT YOU LOVE, NOW ON A GLOBAL STAGE.

▶ YouTube  SUBSCRIBE 🔔

# Brand Up

Your indispensable guide to high-octane success in the modern workplace as you navigate your budding career.

Available at the following retailers

amazon    BARNES&NOBLE    Walmart ›‹·    ⊙TARGET®

**Gail Beltran Nott, CPDC**
Business Coach
Take Wing Coaching

# UNLOCKING POWERFUL INSIGHTS: A ROADMAP FOR BUSINESS OWNERS

By Gail Beltran Nott

As we close the year and prepare for the next, there's a golden opportunity to pause and reflect—not just to set goals or review revenue, but to unlock the insights that will drive your business forward. Your insights are the fusion of experience, expertise, and intuition that transform how you approach challenges and opportunities.

### What is Insight and Why Does It Matter?
Insight is that "a-ha" moment when everything clicks. It emerges when we blend our lived experience, acquired knowledge, and intuitive wisdom. For example, one of my clients was at a crossroads—needing income but longing for more time to pursue their passions. Together, we clarified what brought them fulfillment and shifted their mindset to design a business aligned with their values. Within a year, they partnered with someone who handled the details, allowing them to focus on networking and building relationships--the parts of their business they loved. Now, they're closing five-figure deals and enjoying more time with family and hobbies. "A-ha!"

### The Building Blocks of Insight

### 1. Experience: Lessons from the Past

Our past experiences offer valuable lessons, but their power lies in how we reflect and learn from them. Ask yourself: What challenges have I faced this year and what lessons can I carry forward?

### 2. Expertise: The Power of Applied Learning
Knowledge is crucial but only impactful when it's actionable. Focus on one area of growth for the new year instead of trying to master everything. Distill what you learn into strategies aligned with your unique goals and values.

### 3. Intuition: Trusting Your Inner Guide
Intuition often leads us to solutions beyond logic or data. Cultivating this inner guidance requires trust and practice. Take a moment to reflect on a decision you're facing, breathe deeply, and notice what emerges.

### Cultivating Insights for Your Business
Insight isn't accidental—it's cultivated through intentional reflection, learning, and stillness.

### 1. Reflect on Your Year
Take time to journal about your biggest wins, lessons, and surprises. A favorite exercise of mine is the Vision Reset.

I pause to reassess what's truly important to me and revisit my ideal day and week. Life changes, and so can our vision for how business fits into it.

## 2. Embrace Continuous Learning
Curiosity fuels innovation, but learning without action is just information. Pair every new piece of knowledge with a plan to implement it in your business.

## 3. Practice Stillness and Intuition
In our fast-paced lives, even five minutes of quiet can spark clarity. These quiet moments help us tune into the intuitive wisdom that often leads to breakthroughs.

## Applying Insights to Real-World Challenges
Insights become transformative when applied to decision-making, leadership, and innovation.

## 1. Decision-Making
Use experience, knowledge, and intuition together to evaluate options and find the best path forward.

## 2. Leadership
Tap into insights to connect with your team or clients, anticipate needs, and foster trust.

## 3. Innovation:
Look for unique ways to solve problems that others might overlook.

## Set Intentions with Insight
As you prepare for the new year, let insights guide your intentions. Focus on themes or values instead of rigid resolutions. For me, aligning my business with my values was transformative.

In 2020, I returned to coaching school to become a Certified Professional Diversity Coach. Along the way, I recognized that my earlier definition of success was narrowly focused on financial achievements. Embracing a purpose-driven coaching philosophy, I discovered a deeper sense of fulfillment while empowering my clients to thrive —not only in their purpose but also financially.

## Your Next Steps
Unlocking insights takes practice but it's the key to creating a business and life that resonate with your deeper purpose.

As a coach, I help clients reflect, learn, and act with intention. Together, we turn challenges into opportunities and build businesses that thrive.

This December, don't just set goals—unlock the insights that will make them meaningful. You already have the experience, knowledge, and intuition you need. Let's turn them into your superpower.

If you would like to plan your next 90 days with purpose and intention, download my free 90-Day Business Flight Planner here.

Gail Beltran Nott is a Thought Leadership and Messaging Coach supporting impact entrepreneurs share their expertise and wisdom without perfectionism or performance. Through her Impact Messaging Lab, she helps business owners stop second-guessing, start speaking their truth, and attract aligned clients.

**Connect With Gail**

www.substack.com/@gailnott
www.takewingcoaching.com

**Lisa Nichols**
EFT Tapping Coach
Tapping Into Your True self

# GRATITUDE AS THE BRIDGE BETWEEN THIS YEAR AND THE NEXT

By Lisa Nichols

Whether 2025 was your best year yet, a mix of highs and lows or a total dumpster fire, taking time to reflect with gratitude can be a gift you give yourself as you step into a new year.

**Here's what happens when you look back with the intention to be thankful:**
**You gain a fresh perspective.** When you're in the thick of something, it's easy to focus on what's wrong. Reflecting later can remind you that even in tough situations, there's often something to be grateful for. Maybe you lost someone dear but cherish the time you had together. Or maybe you faced financial stress but are grateful for the small wins that helped you get through it.

**You notice what went right.** Humans love to fixate on the negatives (it's how we're wired), but gratitude challenges that. By focusing on what worked, you'll remember the year more positively—even if it wasn't perfect.

**You find closure.** Gratitude can help you wrap up the year with peace, leaving you ready for whatever's next.

**Here's the thing:** your energy matters.

The universe and your own subconscious respond to what you focus on. Reflecting with gratitude is like placing an order for "more of the good stuff" in life.

**Quick reminder:** Gratitude doesn't mean gaslighting yourself. If something was genuinely hard for you this past year, let yourself feel all the feelings first. Grieve, cry, rage—whatever you need to do. Once you've honored your emotions, you can reflect on what you're grateful for in that experience. Gratitude and truth can coexist.

**Looking Ahead to 2026**
Gratitude isn't just for looking back—it's also a game-changer when it comes to shaping the year ahead. It shifts your mindset from "what's missing" to "what's possible," turning goal setting into something empowering and heart-centered.

**When you set goals with gratitude, here's what happens:**
**You're coming from abundance.** Instead of feeling like you need to fix yourself, your goals are about expanding on what's already good.

**Your goals reflect your values.** Gratitude shows you what you truly care about, so your goals naturally align with what matters most.

**You infuse your goals with positive energy.** Feeling grateful for your dreams as if they've already happened makes them feel real—and achievable.

### Simple Gratitude Practices for Wrapping Up 2025

#### Reflect on the Year.
- Go month by month and list three things you're grateful for from each.
- Look for moments you're proud of, surprises that made you smile, or lessons you gained from challenges.
- Pause after reflecting on each month to really feel the gratitude.

#### Set Grateful Goals for 2026
Write three to five goals that start with gratitude.

#### Examples:
- "I'm grateful for the chance to prioritize my mental health and find balance in 2026."
- "I'm grateful for a body that carries me through life, and I want to care for it by moving it and eating well."
- "I'm grateful for the opportunity to grow my business and share my talents with others."

#### Visualize with Gratitude
Close your eyes and imagine achieving your goals. Feel the joy and gratitude as if they've already happened.

Reflecting with gratitude lets you honor everything 2025 gave you—the good, the bad, and the lessons in between. By carrying that same energy into 2026, you're setting yourself up for a year full of joy, abundance, and meaningful growth.

Let gratitude be the thread that ties your past, present, and future together. The life of your dreams is waiting—and it starts with a simple "Thank You."

# SASSY SELF-CARE

Stop calling it "self-care" like it's optional — call it maintenance. You're a high-value woman, not a clearance-rack afterthought. Rest, hydrate, stretch, say no, and treat your soul like the luxury item it is. Self-care isn't indulgent — it's non-negotiable. Glow-ups aren't accidents — they're habits.

**Danielle Foster**
Founder
The Wellness Affair

# SELF-CARE SUNDAY: BECAUSE BURNOUT IS SO LAST SEASON

By Danielle Foster

Let's face it: life can be a lot. Between work deadlines, endless notifications, and whatever Netflix series you're currently emotionally invested in, it's no wonder self-care often feels like an afterthought. Enter Self-Care Sunday, the one day a week where you unapologetically press pause, pour into your own cup, and remind yourself that you are that woman who deserves peace, balance, and a little bougie pampering.

Now, let's be clear—self-care isn't just bubble baths and face masks (though we love a good eucalyptus bath bomb moment). Real self-care is about tuning in to what you actually need to feel whole, and spoiler: it's not always what Instagram tells you. The beauty of self-care is that it doesn't have to look the same for everyone. It's a deeply personal practice, and the key is finding what resonates with you. So, grab your comfiest robe, a green juice (or mimosa, no judgment), and let's break down how to slay your Self-Care Sunday like the wellness babe you are.

### Step 1: Move Your Body
We're not talking about punishing yourself for the pizza you ate on Friday night. Nope.

Self-care movement is all about feeling good, not looking like a fitness influencer. Start your day with gentle movement. Whether it's a yoga flow, a dance party in your living room, or a lazy stroll to your favorite coffee spot, just get moving. Engaging your body helps release tension and improves circulation. Movement also boosts endorphins, giving you that feel-good energy to carry throughout the day. Bonus points if you're rocking cute leggings while doing it.

### Step 2: Journaling: Reflection of the Mind
Grab a notebook and let the words fly. It doesn't have to be poetic or profound. Write down what's stressing you out, your grocery list, or why your ex's new haircut is offensive. Getting your thoughts out of your head and onto paper is basically a mental detox. Even five minutes of intentional reflection can bring clarity and calm to your mind. Pro tip: end with three things you're grateful for—it's like a gratitude smoothie for your brain.

### Step 3: Tune in and Zone Out
Sound has a powerful impact on our emotional state. Sound baths (totally on the rage right now), calming playlists, or even sitting in silence—

this is the time to give your nervous system a much-needed vacation. (It's been working overtime, honey.) The vibrations from sound therapy can promote healing and reduce stress, creating a sense of harmony within. If sound therapy isn't your jam, just throw on some soothing music, mellow R&B or even a meditation app.

### Step 4: Get Your Snack Game Right
Self-care isn't self-care without snacks. Whip up something nourishing and indulgent. Think avocado toast with a side of chocolate. Or kale chips with... more chocolate. You deserve food that makes you feel good AND tastes good. Period.

### Step 5: Say No Like a Pro
This one's big. Sunday is sacred, which means not feeling bad about turning down brunch invites, work emails, or that friend who always "needs to vent" for three hours. Protect your peace like it's Beyoncé tickets—non-negotiable.

### Step 6: Connect With Your Friends
Self-care doesn't mean isolation. Call your bestie, FaceTime your mom, or schedule a cute coffee date. Sometimes, the best way to recharge is by spending quality time with people who make you feel lighter.

### Step 7: Glow Up Your Space
Light a candle, declutter that corner you've been avoiding, or rearrange your pillows like you're auditioning for HGTV. A cozy, intentional space can do wonders for your mood. Plus, it's the perfect backdrop for a Sunday selfie.

### Final Thoughts: Make it Your Own
Self-Care Sunday isn't just an excuse to take it easy—it's a declaration. It says, "I matter, my needs are valid, and burnout is officially canceled." So, take the day, do what makes you happy, and don't let anyone guilt-trip you into thinking self-care is selfish. It's essential.

By committing to a weekly Self-Care Sunday, you create a ritual that not only enhances your well-being but also reinforces the message that you are worthy of care and attention. Over time, this practice becomes a cornerstone of living a balanced, fulfilled life.

## "Real self-care isn't what Instagram tells you — it's what your soul needs."

So, this Sunday, ask yourself: What does my mind, body, and soul need today? Then give yourself permission to honor the answer. Because true wellness begins with you.

And if anyone questions your Sunday ritual? Smile, take a deep breath, and say, "I'm prioritizing my peace—you should try it sometime."

XOXO
*The wellness Affair*

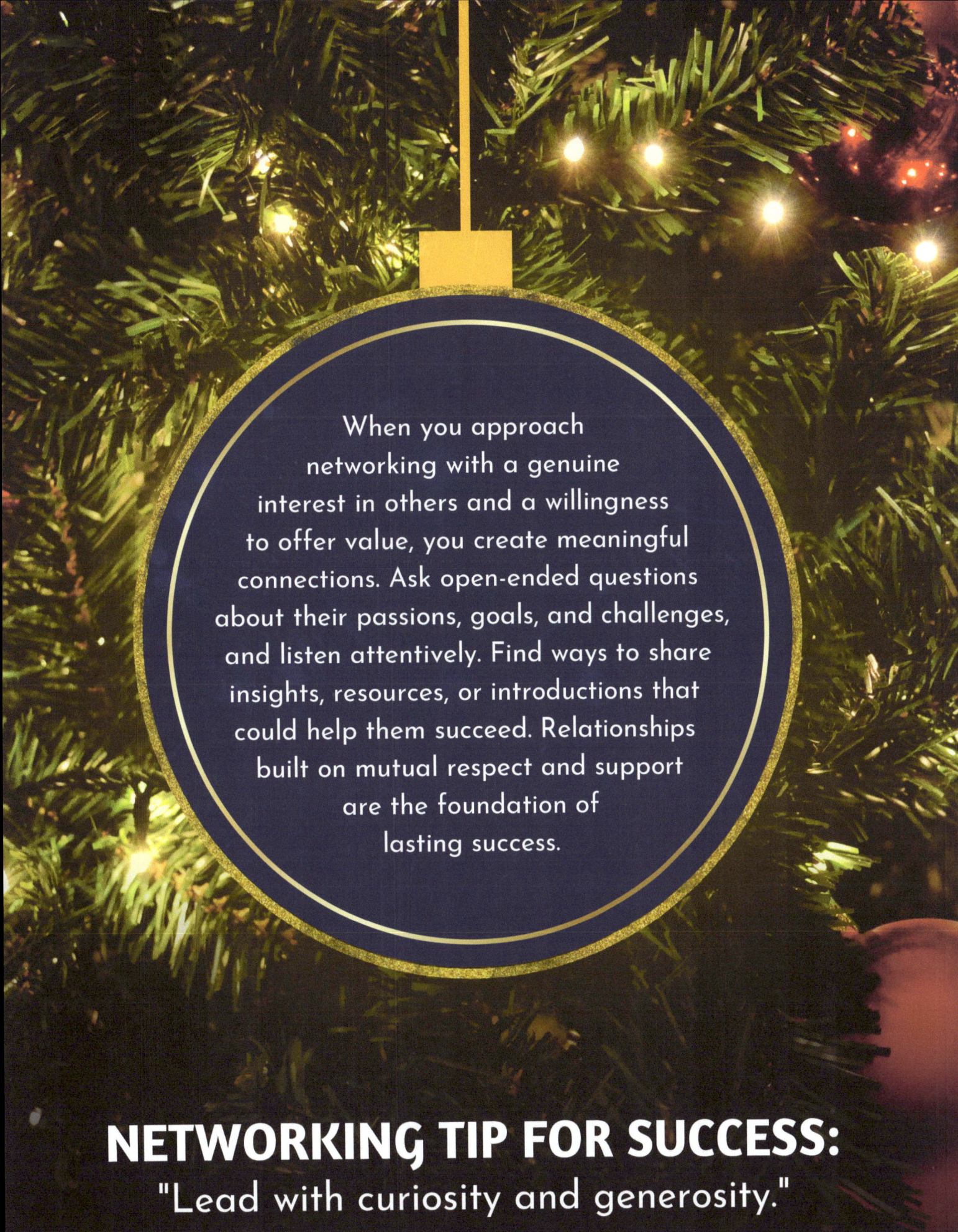

When you approach
networking with a genuine
interest in others and a willingness
to offer value, you create meaningful
connections. Ask open-ended questions
about their passions, goals, and challenges,
and listen attentively. Find ways to share
insights, resources, or introductions that
could help them succeed. Relationships
built on mutual respect and support
are the foundation of
lasting success.

# NETWORKING TIP FOR SUCCESS:
"Lead with curiosity and generosity."

# His
## PERSPECTIVE

**Oleksii Chuiko**

# STOP LIVING A SECONDHAND LIFE: ON THE MERITS OF LOVING YOURSELF

For Norma Bossiuex
By Oleksii Chuiko

When I was approached to write this article, I was cornered by the ultimate question: If I had the *"all eyes on me"* moment, what would I say?

It's an interesting exercise — to pause your ever-busy mind and ask what message is worth sharing. In this era where everyone is an influencer and content floods every corner of the innerweb — huge portions of which are now produced by AI — we're surrounded by videos, artwork, music, poetry, and photography in every imaginable level of quality. The result? It's nearly impossible to rise above the noise.

I often think about how, in the decades before the rise of social media — before 2008 — true geniuses were limited by the tools and reach available to them. Today, in 2025, the opposite is true—your message is no longer limited by access; it's buried beneath an ocean of content and algorithmic sludge.

So if, for just a few fleeting seconds, the entire world paused to listen — and knowing today's attention span gives me only those mere moments — my very concise message would consist of just 2 powerful words...

## Love Yourself

There is no task in life more important than falling in love with yourself.

To understand this statement, we must first define love — and for the sake of brevity, I'll give you the conclusion without the long argument — Love is Understanding.

It's no accident that the Temple of Apollo at Delphi bore the inscription: *"Know thyself."*

To know yourself is to understand yourself. To understand yourself, without harsh judgment, is to love yourself. And that is the beginning of wisdom...the only true way to love others and to change this wild-wild world.

The universe around you is a reflection of your inner self — a projection of your truest being. If you don't love yourself, it becomes impossible to love your life or anyone in it. What you project outward will be distorted, chaotic, and often a reflection of the pain you carry inside. Sadly, you will blame others, circumstances, politicians, the school board, your parents...anyone but the one who has the sole responsibility for your outcomes.

Some might say this perspective sounds self-absorbed, even egotistical. To that I say — Garbage!

The real problem today is that people have become completely *selfless*. Not in the virtuous sense, but in the literal one: they've lost their sense of self. Every day, people spend hours curating photos and videos for social media, seeking validation through likes and hearts of strangers, who, in turn, seek the same. They shape their personalities and preferences to match what others expect — the so-called prime narrative. There is absolutely *no self* left in that.

These endless performances — the obsession with posting every detail of one's life — come from people who haven't truly found or understood themselves. They don't love themselves, so they keep chasing followers rather than seeking substance.

When you genuinely love yourself, you don't need external approval. You don't need applause or admiration. You don't need to *"perform"* for acceptance. Call that *"selfish"* if you want — but a *truly selfish person*, in the highest sense, is *fulfilled*. Their inner void is already filled with love.

A truly *"selfish"* person doesn't take from others to feel whole — they are already whole. They don't drain the room for attention, validation, or praise because their own well is full. Their so-called *"selfishness"* is not a hunger but a fullness; not an act of grasping but of giving without depletion. When you are filled up from within, you overflow. Your presence nourishes rather than consumes. You become the kind of *"selfish"* that heals — because you no longer rely on others to supply what you've already cultivated within yourself.

The emptiness that others try to fill with substances, status, or superficial relationships becomes unnecessary. When love for yourself becomes the foundation of your being, the *projector* of your inner life casts a new and beautiful world — one that not only transforms you but also everyone around you.

Here's the catch—you must *really* fall in love with yourself. No faking it. No half-measures. Don't just *accept* yourself — *love* yourself.

## The Chain of Understanding

You can only love others once you love yourself.
Since love is understanding, when you understand others, you can communicate.
When you can communicate, you can collaborate.
When you collaborate, you can play.
When you play, others want to join you.
When others join you, your circle of influence grows beyond measure.

That's when you become truly powerful.
That's when you become a *real* influencer — not by chasing followers, but by inspiring them.

## The Wisdom of Norma

I'll close with a little wisdom from Norma, my dear friend and adopted grandmother, who is ninety-five years old.

When I first came to the United States, I was lucky to be surrounded by great teachers — Norma was one of the best. Over the past two decades, we've shared countless conversations about life, love, and understanding. We agreed that love is understanding. But what is the opposite of love? Hate? According to Norma *(and I wholeheartedly second this motion),* all negativity originates from *fear*.

A few years ago, she compiled a list of insights — simple truths that she shares with anyone willing to listen during her daily walks on the West Cliff of Santa Cruz.

If love is understanding, then fear is ignorance.
Faith, she would say, is *the absence of doubt*.
Forgiveness is *self-serving*.
Egotism is *limitation*.
Happiness is *fleeting*. Joy is a *state of mind*.
Consciousness is *the right action at the right time*.
And evil? Evil is simply *the lack of self-love*.

So the next time you find yourself looking into the mirror at the masterpiece staring back, don't be a jerk — smile, and with passion proudly proclaim: *"I Love Me."*

*Oleksii Chuiko is first and foremost a father and husband, then a community leader, marketing & communications strategist, and an unapologetic optimist who believes in living deliberately and laughing often. When he's not running organizations or hosting events, you'll probably find him running amok in the mosh pit at your local punk show.*

**Connect With Oleksii**

oc@joinshriners.org
www.linkedin.com/in/oleksii-chuiko

# MAN VS. MYTH

Stereotype Debunk: Emotional Expression & Male Friendship

## MYTH:

### Men don't talk about feelings

For generations, this idea has shaped how we view masculinity — as silent, stoic, and emotionally distant. From locker rooms to boardrooms, boys are told to "man up," not open up.

## REALITY CHECK:

### 68%

of men say they want deeper friendships.

Despite the stereotype, most men crave emotional depth and meaningful connection. Emotional silence isn't hardwired — it's cultural. It's learned. And it's slowly being unlearned.

## THE SHIFT

Men are building emotional vocabularies. They're opening up in therapy, sharing on group chats, and creating podcasts that normalize vulnerability. The need has always been there — what's changing is the permission to express it.

# CONSISTENCY BUILDS CONFIDENCE

Success rarely comes from one breakthrough moment. It's built in the quiet repetition, the follow-throughs, the habits, and the daily choices no one applauds. Every time you keep your word, meet a deadline, or show up even when it's inconvenient, you strengthen the foundation beneath your goals. That foundation becomes confidence. And confidence turns momentum into mastery.

**Brian "Cowboy" Sanchez**
Entrepreneur/Philanthropist

# NAVIGATING THE BALANCING ACT: A MAN'S PERSPECTIVE ON FATHERHOOD, MARRIAGE, AND PROVIDING

By Brian "Cowboy" Sanchez

In today's fast-paced world, the modern man often finds himself wearing multiple hats. Father, husband, provider, entrepreneur, and community volunteer. Balancing these roles isn't just about time management; it's about aligning priorities, nurturing relationships, and maintaining personal well-being. Here's a deeper dive into how to juggle these responsibilities effectively, especially during the bustling holiday season.

### Embracing the Role of a Father
Fatherhood is a profound journey filled with moments that shape both the child and the parent. The key is presence. Being physically there is important, but emotional availability is what truly matters. Engage in daily rituals like bedtime stories, weekend activities, or simple conversations about their day. These moments foster lasting bonds while teaching children about love, resilience, and integrity through example.

### Strengthening the Marital Bond
Marriage is the partnership that often forms the foundation for balancing other life roles. Communication is the cornerstone. Regular check-ins with your spouse to discuss feelings, challenges, and goals help maintain connection. Date nights, even if they're simple home dinners

after the kids are asleep, can reignite intimacy and companionship.

### Providing: Beyond Financial Stability
Being a provider extends beyond finances. It's about creating a secure and nurturing environment. This includes contributing to household responsibilities, supporting your family's emotional needs, and planning for future aspirations. Financial provision is important, but emotional and psychological support are equally vital.

### Managing a Business and Career Ambitions
Running a business or advancing in a career demands dedication. The secret is delegation and boundaries. Trust your team, prioritize tasks, and don't hesitate to say no when necessary. Efficient time management tools and practices, like digital calendars and productivity apps, can streamline work commitments, freeing up time for family.

### The Spirit of Volunteering During the Holidays
The holidays are a season of giving — not just of gifts, but of time, kindness, and compassion. While volunteering can feel like *one more thing* on an already full plate, inviting your family to take part turns it into something far more meaningful. It's a chance to create memories, connect with each other,

and give back to the community — while teaching your children what it means to cultivate a heart of service and step up when others need a hand.

Whether it's serving meals at a shelter or organizing charity events, these activities teach children compassion and gratitude while strengthening family ties.

### Self-Care: The Overlooked Priority

Balance isn't sustainable without self-care. Regular exercise, hobbies, and downtime are crucial. Mental health practices, like meditation or journaling, can provide clarity and reduce stress. Remember, taking care of yourself isn't selfish; it's necessary to be the best version of yourself for others.

### Conclusion

Balancing fatherhood, marriage, providing, career ambitions, and community involvement is undoubtedly challenging. However, with intentionality, open communication, and a focus on what truly matters, it's not only possible but deeply fulfilling. Embrace the journey, celebrate small victories, and remember that perfection isn't the goal. Presence, purpose, and love are.

# happy holidays

FROM *Sass* n' SOUL

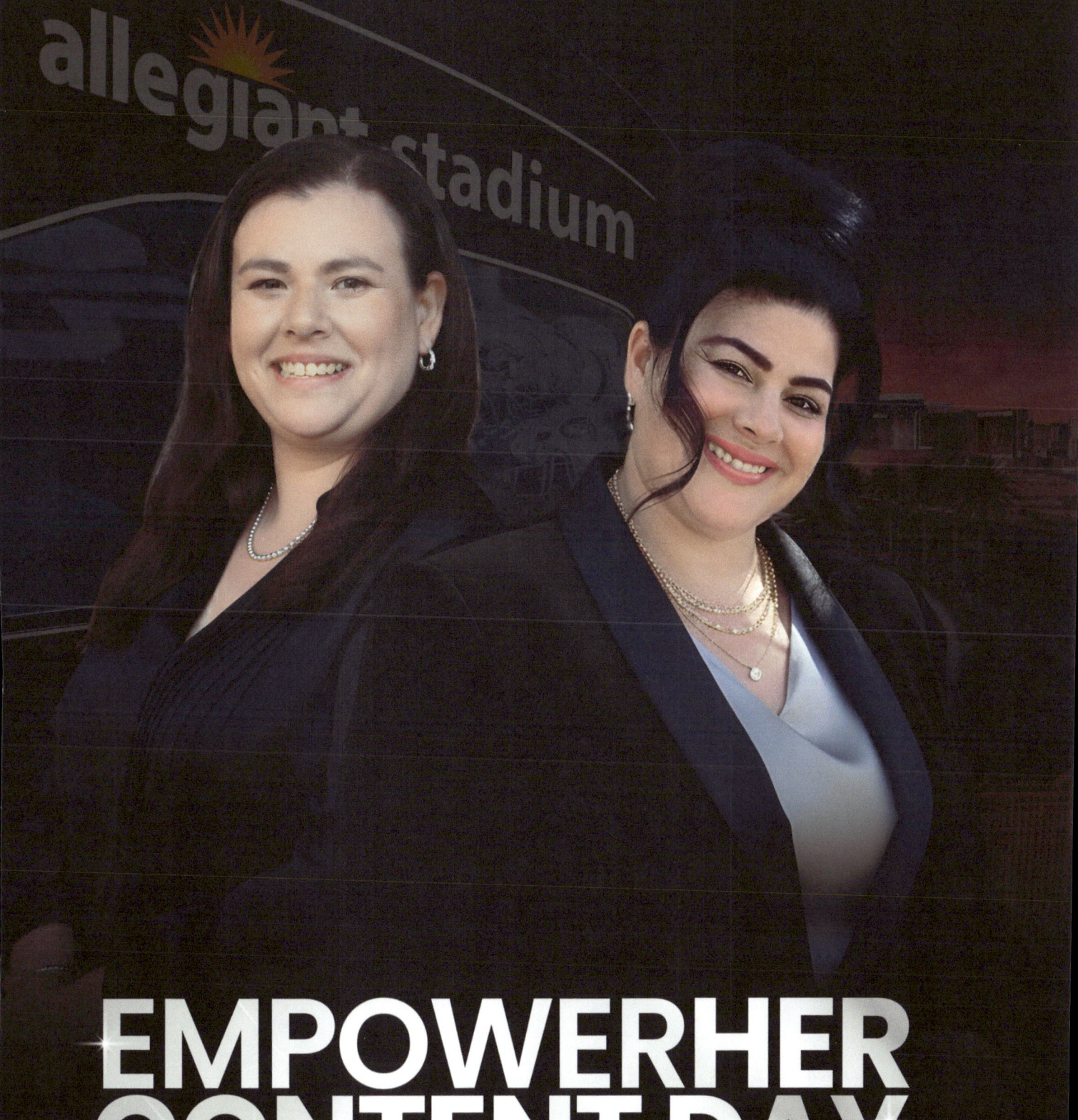

# EMPOWERHER
# CONTENT DAY

ONE STADIUM, 40,000 WOMEN, INFINITE IMPACT

"Living a Legendary Life doesn't come from grand, heroic gestures, but from the small, consistent actions that transform hearts."

Cyndee Paulson-Heer

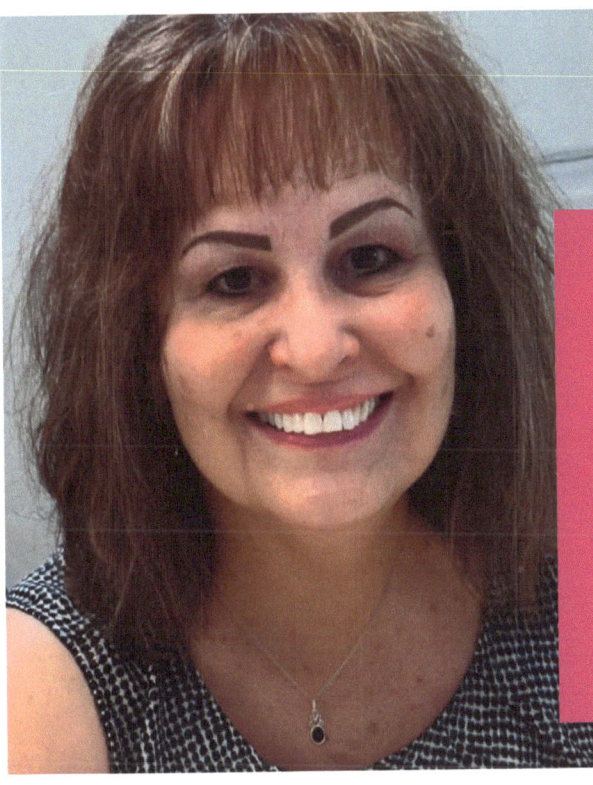

**Cyndee Paulson-Heer**
Founder, Sass n' Soul Magazine &
CyndeePaulsonHeer.com
Author • Speaker • Women's Empowerment Advocate

Cyndee Paulson-Heer is a thought leader in
authenticity, Leadership, and self-actualization.
Through Sass n' Soul and CyndeePaulsonHeer.com she
inspires women to live intentionally, lead with integrity,
and create legacies of purpose and impact.

*CyndeePaulsonHeer.com*
"Live as though you are legend."

Thank you to our extraordinary contributors for investing more than time and talent. Thank you for pouring your life energy into these pages. Your words are more than articles; they are offerings—crafted to educate, uplift, and spark something meaningful in every reader who turns these pages.

It is my hope that the insights you've shared will create a ripple far beyond the ink. You've added not just content, but the depth of your intellect and soul, helping build a publication designed to inspire women—and a few good men—to grow, rise, and lead with purpose.

Because of you, these pages don't simply communicate.
They ignite.
They teach.
They transform.

Thank you for lending your voice, your wisdom, and the irreplaceable essence of who you are. Sass n' Soul is richer because of your contribution—and our readers are, too. This collaboration is a tapestry woven by many hands, and I am grateful for every thread.

I'd also like to extend my heartfelt thanks to Hanna Olivas and Adriana Luna Carlos for helping make this publication possible through She Rises Studios. Your belief in this project and your commitment to empowering women created the doorway that allowed Sass n' Soul to step into print.

And last—but certainly never least—my deepest appreciation goes to my amazing cousin, DeeDee Buserwinni. When she's not hiking through cell-service dead zones, she somehow still manages to prioritize proofreading for Sass n' Soul—catching everything from missing or mischievous commas to those extra words that sneak in when ideas run faster than typing fingers. She refines, clarifies, punctuates, and polishes with a level of care that elevates every page.